Christmas Favorites

Collected by
Mary Ann Crouch and
Jan Stedman

The Holiday Handbook

decorating
entertaining
and
recipes

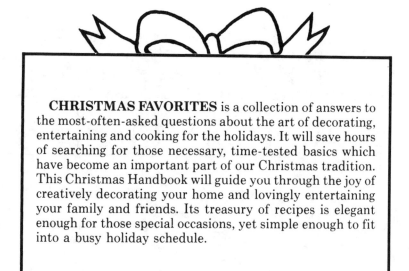

CHRISTMAS FAVORITES is a collection of answers to the most-often-asked questions about the art of decorating, entertaining and cooking for the holidays. It will save hours of searching for those necessary, time-tested basics which have become an important part of our Christmas tradition. This Christmas Handbook will guide you through the joy of creatively decorating your home and lovingly entertaining your family and friends. Its treasury of recipes is elegant enough for those special occasions, yet simple enough to fit into a busy holiday schedule.

THANKS!!

● to friends and relatives who have through the years so willingly shared their favorite recipes...many of which we can no longer remember the source.

● to customers and garden club audiences whose many questions about Christmas decorating inspired us to organize the answers and write them down.

● to Lulie Mallard, Harriet Martin and Page Renger for their professional assistance.

● to Leigh McArtan for the cover design.

● to our husbands and children who somehow survived gross neglect while we put this book together.

First printing, November 1983, 5,000 copies
Second printing, May 1984, 10,000 copies
Third printing, October 1984, 10,000 copies
Fourth printing, September 1985, 15,000 copies
Fifth printing, September 1986, 20,000 copies
Sixth printing, September 1987, 20,000 copies
Seventh printing, October 1988, 20,000 copies
Eighth printing, July 1990, 20,000 copies
Ninth printing, August 1991, 30,000 copies
Tenth printing, August 1992, 30,000 copies
Eleventh printing, July 1996, 30,000 copies

Library of Congress Catalog Number 83-91210

Printed in the USA by

WIMMER
The Wimmer Companies, Inc.
Memphis

TABLE OF CONTENTS

RECIPES

TAKE TIME TO "CATCH THE SPIRIT"

Watch the fire
Toast marshmallows by the fire
Eat fudge
Pull taffy
Read your favorite Christmas story
Look at family scrapbooks
Cry a little
Sing carols
Look for the Star of Bethlehem
Make snow ice cream
Visit a lonely friend
Call a favorite relative
Take each child individually to **his** favorite place for lunch
Go "stocking stuffing" shopping with your husband — hold hands
DON'T MISS THE CHRISTMAS SERVICE AT YOUR CHURCH

Decorating

More than at any other time of the year, your home should reflect genuine hospitality and the warmth of the season, for Christmas is a special time for family and friends. "Deck the halls with boughs of holly . . . ", a welcoming wreath on the front door and a decorated tree. These traditionally basic decorating principles and techniques are easily adapted to individual tastes. They are designed to stimulate your imagination and to make decorating easy and fun.

NATURAL MATERIALS

WORKING WITH FRESH GREENERY

Fresh greenery has been an important part of the American Christmas tradition since the arrival of the first English settlers. With them they brought the ancient English custom of exchanging boughs of evergreens as a sign of unending friendship. We have adapted and expanded this tradition to include fresh greenery in many of our decorations. These few simple instructions will add beauty, luster and long life to the greenery you select.

Selection: Select greenery with thick leaves and waxy foliage such as boxwood, laurel, magnolia, holly, osmanthus, rhododendron, aucuba or pittosporum. Evergreens such as hemlock, cedar, pine and fir also hold up well after cutting. Cut stems at a 45° angle and, when cutting, be careful not to ruin the shape of your tree or shrub.

Conditioning: Conditioning takes a little extra time, but it is worth the effort.
1. Slightly crush stem-ends of larger greenery with a hammer or pliers.
2. Submerge all greenery overnight in water. Magnolia should be soaked several days. Weight it down with bricks if necessary. Do not allow the water to freeze.
3. Dry foliage thoroughly with absorbent paper.
4. Seal, using one of several methods:
   a. Dip in clear, liquid floor wax.
   b. Spray with a cheap, sticky hair spray.
   c. Spray with a clear, high-gloss acrylic spray or varnish.
5. Allow foliage to dry and it is then ready to use in your arrangements, wreaths or decorations. Conditioning will add luster to the foliage and several extra weeks' beauty to the greenery.

DANGER!! Some holiday greenery including yew, mistletoe berries, holly berries, Jerusalem cherries and some poinsettia leaves are poisonous. Keep them away from small children!!

CAUTION: Pine and cedar resin will stain walls, floors, furniture and fabric, so dip the stem ends in candle wax or paraffin to seal.

Preserving and Turning Foliage Brown: Add variety to your Christmas decorations with laurel, camellia, eucalyptus or magnolia leaves, dried to a rich brown color in a glycerine solution:

1 part glycerine or anti-freeze
2 parts warm water

Directions: Branches: 1. Make vertical cuts 1 inch into the tips of the branches, or smash tips; submerge the ends in 2-3 inches of the solution of glycerine and warm water. 2. Watch mixture and keep adding enough solution to keep 2 inches of stem covered. 3. The leaves will dry a soft brown and be ready in 2-3 weeks.
Individual Leaves: When treating individual leaves, they must be covered completely. Weight them down in the solution if necessary. The leaves will turn and be ready in 10 days. When they are completely dry, spray with hair spray or a clear acrylic spray for additional protection and luster.

WORKING WITH FRESH FRUITS AND BERRIES

Selection: Consider the weight of the fruit and how it is to be used in decorating. Select fruit and berries just as they become ripe — **not** when they are soft, spotted or over-ripe.

Conditioning: Holiday fruit and berries will last much longer if they are sealed. All surfaces must be covered thoroughly. Several methods may be used for sealing as well as for a glossy finish:

  I. Spray with Pam. This method is primarily used for fruit that is to be eaten later. Be sure to clean and dry fruit before spraying.

  II. Dip in a clear floor wax. Dry on waxed paper. This is the best method for cut fruit such as apple halves or for berries and is also the easiest and least expensive.

III. Spray with hair spray, a clear high-gloss acrylic spray or a clear lacquer. Allow to dry thoroughly. Fruit may need several coats. (Fruit treated with methods II and III **may not** be eaten!!)

Preparing for Use in Decorations:

Fruit: 1. Force a piece of strong florist wire through the center of the fruit, crosswise. 2. Pull the wire ends evenly to the base of the fruit. At this point some fruit may be wired around the base of the wreath or garland. 3. For a more secure hold, force the blunt end of a 3-inch wooden florist pick into the base of the fruit. Twist the wire in the fruit tightly around the pick.

DANGER!! The dye in some florist picks is poisonous. **Do not eat fruit that has been punctured with a florist pick!**

Berries: Condition berries as you would fruit, using method II or III. Dry thoroughly (usually overnight). Berry clusters may be attached to decorations with U-shaped fern pins or the stems may be wired on florist picks.

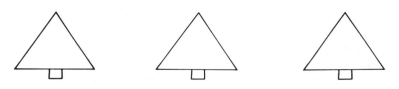

WORKING WITH NUTS, SEEDS, PINE CONES AND PODS

Selection: Magnolia seedpods, pine cones, nuts, sweet gum balls, cotton bolls, lotus pods and a variety of other seed pods add texture and interest to Christmas decorations.

Conditioning:
1. Bake pine cones, nuts and other pods in a 150°-200° oven for about 2 hours to kill insects and worms.
2. Spray magnolia seed pods or anything with loose seeds with an inexpensive, sticky hair spray or with spray glue.
3. For a glossy effect, spray all items with hairspray, a clear acrylic spray or clear lacquer. A glossy wood tone spray adds a little color and is especially good on pine cones, nuts, sweet gum balls and darker pods.

Preparing for Use in Decorations: Pine cones, nuts and pods may be secured to decorations in many ways. In some wreaths or in permanent decorations, gluing with a hot glue gun is quickest. When this is not possible, use one of the following methods:

Pine Cones: 1. Wrap a piece of florist wire completely around the lower scales between the layers. 2. Twist wire; pull one wire half-way back around cone until the two wires are opposite each other; pull the two ends to the base of the cone and twist again. 3. Wrap the wires around the base of the decoration, or twist around a wooden florist pick.

Pine Cone Flowers: With a small saw or hog-nose hedge shears, cut across and through the pine cone above the 4th or 5th row of scales. The bottom portion will look like a flower and may be wired for decorations, just like the pine cone.

Nuts and Sweet Gum Balls:

    Method I — Glue directly on the decoration with a hot glue gun or other fast-drying glue when possible — this is the easiest method.

    Method II — Small holes may be drilled in nuts and a small florist pick glued in the hole. For sweet gum balls, force the florist pick into the ball and glue to secure.

    Method III — Place nut in a 4″ square of nylon stocking material. Pull the nylon material tightly around the nut. (The sheer nylon will not show on the nut.) Secure the nylon by twisting with the small wire that is attached to a wooden florist pick. Trim the excess nylon away from base. Finish by wrapping wire and the ends of nylon with brown florist tape.

Storage: To store decorations of cones or nuts, place in a plastic bag with a few moth balls to discourage insects.

WORKING WITH DRIED HERBS, FLOWERS AND GRASSES

Natural materials such as herbs and flowers may be picked in the summer and fall and dried for use during the holidays. Don't forget the possibilities of those wild flowers and grasses found along the road side . . . fondly nicknamed "Roadsidea." "Roadsidea" varies in each section of the country and offers an interesting variety for creative decorating: goldenrod, wheat, cattails, Queen Anne's Lace, pussy willow, etc. Be sure to remember family allergies when selecting them for fresh arrangements or for drying. There are several methods for drying herbs, flowers and "Roadsidea." Listed are the most common methods for each, but these methods may be interchanged. Hydrangea, yarrow and straw flowers do well with the "hang drying" method used for herbs, and the flowers of some herbs need the conditioning of a drying medium. These are basic guidelines, so pick extras and experiment. Drying your own is inexpensive and fun, but it is still easier and worth the extra cost to purchase some materials, such as statice, baby's breath or eucalyptus.

DANGER!! Never put **any** dried materials near a candle or flame!

Selection: Harvest flowers and herbs for drying early in the morning before the dew has dried. Select ones that are open, fresh-looking and have not started to fade. Seed heads are best just before they open.

Drying Methods

I. **Herbs — Hang-drying:** 1. Tie the stem ends of a bunch of one kind of herb together with a string. 2. Hang upside down in a dry, warm place away from the sunlight. 3. Be sure the air can circulate all around to prevent mildew. 4. "Hang-drying" is perhaps the oldest method of drying and takes about 2 weeks. Dry the herb's flowers as you would any other flowers. (When making wreaths of fresh herbs, allow them to dry on the wreath. See directions for "Herb Wreaths".)

II. **Flowers — Drying in a Medium:** The best way to preserve the color and shape of flowers is to bury them in a drying medium. An inexpensive medium is made of half household borax powder and half cornmeal (fine grain, dry sand may be substituted for cornmeal). Finely crushed silica gel crystals or other drying mixtures may be purchased at flower shops. They are more expensive but result in truer, brighter colors. 1. Cut the stems off the freshly picked flowers. 2. Use a pin or wire to make a small hole in the center of the head where the stem was removed. You will use this hole later for attaching the stem wire. (Some people attach the wire at this point, but it makes drying more difficult.) 3. Pour about 3 inches of drying medium into a flat container with a tight-fitting lid. 4. Place flowers upright in medium, taking care that they do not touch each other. 5. Slowly pour more medium all around flowers and between every petal and leaf. 6. Cover each layer of flowers with drying medium. The deeper the container, the more layers you may add. 7. Cover the top layer with several more inches of the medium. 8. Seal tightly and put in a dry, warm place. 9. Check after 3 days. Drying time varies with the density of the flower petals and the medium used. Flowers dried in sand take the longest — up to 3 weeks. 10. When flowers feel dry and crisp, remove carefully, and gently brush or shake off all drying medium. 11. With clear, white craft glue, glue florist stem wire into hole made earlier in the center of the head. 12. To finish, wrap wire stem with green florist tape and attach leaves, artificial or dried, as you wrap.

NOTE: Hydrangea, yarrow, statice, goldenrod, baby's breath and straw flowers may be dried by "Hang-drying."

III. **"Roadsidea" — Drying in the Field:**
1. If left alone, "Roadsidea" will usually dry right on its stems in the field. 2. Strip off unwanted dried leaves. 3. Since most colors fade when dried in the sun, use floral spray paint to add color, or for a good mixture of texture, color and size, purchase a few brightly colored additions. 4. Spray with hair spray or a clear acrylic or lacquer to prevent shedding.

NOTE: "Hang-drying" is also a successful method for some "Roadsidea." Larger wild flowers require a drying medium.

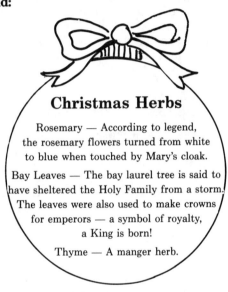

Christmas Herbs

Rosemary — According to legend, the rosemary flowers turned from white to blue when touched by Mary's cloak.

Bay Leaves — The bay laurel tree is said to have sheltered the Holy Family from a storm. The leaves were also used to make crowns for emperors — a symbol of royalty, a King is born!

Thyme — A manger herb.

WORKING WITH MOSSES

The natural mosses have become popular with the increased use of natural materials at Christmas.

Selection: Treated planter's moss (green sheet moss)* is usually best purchased in a Christmas or flower shop, but Spanish moss is easy to gather and condition yourself. Select clean Spanish moss without leaves, sticks or trash. Watch for small animals and insects.

*If you live in the mountains and want to try digging your own, lift moss from the ground with as little dirt as possible. Spread in a single layer to dry. When dry, shake off any remaining loose dirt.

Conditioning: 1. Put Spanish moss in a plastic bag large enough to hold it loosely. 2. Spray the moss well with insect spray. 3. Quickly seal the bag tightly. 4. Leave several days, and it will be ready to use.

DANGER!! Spanish moss burns easily. Keep away from candles.

WREATHS AND BOWS

The age-old custom of a circle of greenery to symbolize never-ending hope and eternal love continues to be an important part of Christmas today. The sizes and materials are varied, but through the years the favorite wreaths continue to fall into a few basic categories. A green wreath, fresh or permanent, is the traditional favorite. Other natural materials, such as pine cones, vines, corn shucks, moss, straw and dried materials, compose another popular category. Fabric and bow wreaths can be a colorful decoration and are easy to vary with different coordinated fabrics and ribbons. Novelty wreaths, such as an edible candy or cookie wreath for visiting children or even a dog biscuit wreath for "Fido's" house, make creating fun.

ALL-TIME FAVORITES!!

1. **Greenery Wreaths:**   **Fresh Greenery**
                                  Permanent Greenery
2. **Natural Dried Material Wreaths:**
                                  Pine Cone, Nut and Pod
                                  Corn Shuck
                                  Straw
                                  Eucalyptus
                                  Dried Flower, Herb and Grass
                                  Spice
                                  Vine
                                  Moss
3. **Fabric and Ribbon Wreaths**
4. **Novelty Wreaths:**   **Edible**
                                  Toy and Gadget
                                  Personalized

Basic Materials Needed for Most Wreaths:
1. Chenille stem for hanger — color to match finished wreath
2. Fern pins (U-shaped florist pins)
3. Narrow gage florist wire — #24 or #22
4. 3-inch wooden florist picks with wires
5. Roll of green florist tape
6. Good pair of wire cutters and clippers for fresh greenery
7. Scissors
8. Wreath form — For most wreaths, use a straw form; it is sturdier, will not break and can be reused. Items stuck into a straw form are more secure. Styrofoam forms are best for the fabric ruffled wreath and for those wound with ribbon or fabric. When selecting the wreath form size, remember that a picked wreath, when it is finished, will be about 6 inches larger than the form. A 16-inch wreath form, when picked with greenery, is a good size for most doors. Leave the green plastic on straw form for a green wreath. For beige-colored wreaths, such as corn shuck or dried baby's breath, remove the plastic.

Basic Design Ideas:
1. Combine several different types of greenery for depth and contrast.
2. Place largest greens on wreath first.
3. When selecting materials, consider the color and style of your home and the place where the wreath will be hung. Colors should blend but contrast to stand out against the background.
4. Remember to leave room for a bow. Don't waste material that will not show behind a bow.
5. When adding large items such as fruit or pine cones, use an odd number.

NOTE: Lightweight wreaths may be hung on glass storm doors with suction-cup hangers.

‼ FIRST THINGS FIRST ‼

(Putting a Hanger on the Wreath) A "wad of wire" used as a hanger is a disaster and can distract from an otherwise attractive wreath. Put the hanger on **first** since roughly handling the finished wreath could damage it. Follow these directions for a strong, professional-looking hook:

Directions: 1. Determine where hook is to be located. 2. Force a screwdriver through the back of the straw form at a slight angle. 3. Insert a 9-inch piece of chenille stem (one that will match finished wreath) through the hole. 4. Twist together ends of stem about ½ inch from the ends to make a large loop. 5. Fold each of the two ½-inch ends back in opposite directions and twist around main part of loop. 6. Pull twisted area into wreath form. 7. Twist loop several times at the base of the wreath form to make a smaller loop. 8. Secure loop with a fern pin, so it will not slip.

GREENERY WREATHS

BASIC WREATH WITH FRESH GREENERY

Straw wreath form (usually 16-inch for front door)
Fern pins — 50
3-inch green wooden florist picks
Fresh greenery (conditioned)*
Green florist tape (optional)
Green chenille stem for hanger

Directions: 1. Put hanger on wreath form. 2. Using fern pins, secure largest (no larger than 4 or 5 inches) conditioned greenery (or leaves, if using magnolia) to the wreath first. (*For conditioning directions, see "Working with Fresh Greenery.")

Cover sides and front. It will look "flat" until smaller pieces are added, but this method covers quickly and easily. 3. Twist the wire of the wooden picks around the smaller pieces of greenery. Insert picks into wreath at a slight angle or straight up. This adds depth to the wreath. If a bow is to be added, leave room for the bow.

Favorite Additions: Add individual touches with fruit, berries, seed pods and pine cones. Attach them with fern pins, wire or florist picks, as indicated in preceding instructions on preparing and conditioning. (See "Working With Fresh Fruits and Berries" and "Working With Nuts, Seeds, Pine Cones and Pods.")

BASIC WREATH WITH PERMANENT GREENERY

Straw wreath form (14-inch or 16-inch)
Permanent pine, holly or boxwood garland —
(1 garland for 14-inch wreath; 1 garland plus
2 dozen matching picks for 16-inch wreath)
Fern pins — about 50
Green chenille stem
Bow

Directions: 1. Attach chenille stem hanger. 2. Beginning in the center of the outside edge of the wreath form, where the bow will be attached, attach the garland with a fern pin (U-shaped florist pin). Pull garland completely around the outside of the wreath form and pin with fern pins about every 3 inches. Be careful to pull greenery out and not let it get pinned underneath. 3. When the wreath has been circled, clip the garland with wire cutters and follow the same procedure for the top of the wreath. 4. Clip again and use remaining garland for inside edge. 5. When using a 16-inch form, use matching picks to finish covering the form (about 2 dozen). 6. Be sure to leave a space for the bow. 7. Attach your favorite decorations. 8. Attach the bow.

Favorite Additions: This is a very versatile wreath. Small toys, artificial fruit, pine cones, ornaments, bows and dried flowers all make handsome additions. Our favorite wreath combines apples, pine cones and baby's breath. If you need a waterproof wreath, this one is ideal. Be sure, however, that the added decorations and the bow are also of waterproof materials.

Revitalizing Used Artificial Greenery and Fruit: Most plastic decorations may be washed with cool water and a mild detergent. Dry thoroughly. For a new luster, spray with a clear acrylic spray. If the color has faded, "antique" the greenery or fruit with a glossy wood-tone acrylic or lacquer spray. When "antiquing" the entire wreath or arrangement, it is easier and more economical to spray it **after** the decoration is complete. "Antiquing" is also a good trick for slightly worn wooden ornaments. For a special "old-world" look, sprinkle with diamond dust while the spray is still wet.

Advent* Wreaths: Use the same method of making other green wreaths, but completely cover the wreath form with greenery. If using fresh greenery, protect the table by putting the wreath down flat on a piece of green cardboard or felt that has been cut "wreath size".

Space 4 candle holders (candle holders with metal picks are available at candle or Christmas shops) evenly around the wreath, and place a short candle holder in the center to hold the 5th candle. A candle is lighted each Sunday for 4 Sundays before Christmas and the 5th is lighted on Christmas Eve. Candle colors and certain types of greenery used on the wreath have special symbolic meanings. Since Advent traditions vary widely, request a copy of devotional thoughts, customs and ideas from your church.

*Advent is the four weeks period preceding Christmas. The word "advent" means coming. For Christians this is a time of anticipation and preparation for Christmas and the birth of Christ.

WREATHS WITH NATURAL DRIED MATERIALS

Wreaths with natural dried materials are a beautiful, year-round addition to homes with country or colonial decor. More of these materials are becoming available in stores. If you enjoy collecting and conditioning your own, however, follow directions given in Chapter I, "Natural Materials."

PINE CONE, SEED POD AND NUT WREATH

Conditioned pine cones, pods or nuts*
(enough to cover wreath form)
Straw wreath form (a wire one may be
used for pine cones)
Beige or brown chenille stem for hanger
3-inch wooden florist picks with wires

A variety of cones, nuts and pods from different types of trees make attractive wreaths. Cover an entire wreath with just one type cone or select an interesting mixture. The unusual Charleston, South Carolina, low-country "Pop Corn Wreath" utilizes clusters of seed pods of the Chinese Tallow Tree. Wreaths of cotton bolls, sweet gum balls and pine cones are also Southern favorites.

Directions: Method I — Picks: 1. Remove the green plastic from the straw wreath form. 2. Attach the hanger. 3. Twist the wires of wooden florist picks around the small clusters of seeds and pods or around the nylon hosiery material encasing the nuts.* The wire of the wired pine cones is also twisted on wooden picks. 4. Insert picks into the wreath form at an angle. 5. Cover wreath completely. 6. Attach bow.
*See "Working with Nuts, Seeds, Pine Cones and Pods" for instructions for selecting, conditioning and preparing for decorating.

Method II — Glue: With a hot glue gun, glue cones, nuts or pods to a wreath form, attaching the largest ones first. Fill spaces with smaller items such as sweet gum balls. If a glue gun is not available, use linoleum glue.

Method III — Wire Forms: There is a special wire form made for heavier pine cone wreaths. They are available at Christmas shops or greenhouses. To make these wreaths, the pine cones are soaked in water for about an hour so they will close. The base of each cone is then forced into the wire frame until several rows of scales have been pushed through the wire. Put the wreath in a warm dry place, and as the cones dry and open, they will be attached securely to the wire frame and the wreath will be full and tight. If needed, secure any loose ones with a piece of florist wire. When the wreath is completely dry (several days), spray with a clear varnish or a glossy wood tone spray for a gloss and a richer color.

CORN SHUCK WREATH

16-inch straw wreath form
8-ounce package cornhusks*
Beige chenille stem for hanger
3-inch wooden florist picks with wires

Directions: 1. Select conditioned cornhusks.* Moisten, if necessary, until they are pliable and bend without breaking. Wider pieces may need to be split lengthwise. 2. Remove green plastic from wreath form. 3. Attach chenille stem hanger.

 4. Make loops of the cornhusk strips by folding over and securing the two ends together. Wrap the wires of the florist picks around the ends. 5. Insert picks into the wreath at an angle. 6. Working in the same direction, fill the wreath form with overlapping rows of husk loops. 7. Add your own touch with a bow, cornhusk ornament or other natural decorations.

Favorite Additions: A calico or gingham bow and ornaments, pine cones, bunches of baby's breath tucked between rows of cornhusk loops, a cornhusk angel or a bunch of wheat for a "country look."

***Cornhusks:** Purchase a bag of treated cornhusks at a craft or Christmas shop. This is **much** easier than conditioning your own; they are usually prettier and are inexpensive. One 8-ounce package is enough for a 16-inch wreath. If, however, they are not available in your area, you may dry green ones on a screen wire in the sun or select ones that are already sun-bleached and dried on the ear. For a lighter color, soak them in a mixture of water and a little household bleach. Spread husks, without overlapping, to dry thoroughly.

BASIC STRAW WREATH

Straw wreath form
Beige chenille stem for hanger
Ribbon for strip-winding and bow
2 U-shaped fern pins

The easiest and least expensive wreath is simply a straw wreath form with a bow and a few simple decorations. It is the base for many novelty and "country" wreaths and is easy enough for children to make.

Directions: 1. Remove green plastic from wreath form. 2. Attach hanger. 3. Strip-wind wreath with ribbon to match the bow. "Strip-winding" is evenly winding the ribbon around the wreath, leaving spaces between with the straw showing. Attach one end of the ribbon with a fern pin to the back of the wreath form where the bow is to be placed. Wind ribbon around the wreath, leaving about 1 to 3 inches of straw (depending on wreath size) between each looping of ribbon. End where you began, and attach second end with another fern pin. Strip-winding a 16-inch wreath takes 3 yards; a 14-inch wreath, 2½ yards; and a 12-inch wreath, 2 yards. 4. Add a bow or decorations of your choice. See "Bow Making" instructions for the amount of additional ribbon needed for a bow.

EUCALYPTUS WREATH

16-inch straw wreath form
1-pound bunch of eucalyptus (size of bunches vary; this
amount needed)
3-inch wooden florist picks with wires
Chenille stem for hanger

Directions: 1. Remove the green plastic from the wreath form and attach hanger. 2. Using garden shears, cut eucalyptus in a variety of lengths from 3 inches to 5 inches. (Cut the stems close to the pair of leaves for the top of each piece. This makes it more attractive.) 3. Wrap the wire of a florist pick around 3 sprigs. 4. Insert the picks into the straw wreath at an angle. Work in the same direction around the wreath form until it is covered. 5. Add a bow if desired.

 Favorite Additions: Pine cones, small bunches of baby's breath or other dried materials. Add a bunch of deep red or wine artificial berries to a blue eucalyptus wreath.

BASIC DRIED WREATH WITH FLOWERS, HERBS AND GRASSES
(Baby's Breath or Statice Wreath)

14-inch or 16-inch straw wreath form
3-inch wooden florist picks with wires (natural
color is best, if available)
Beige chenille stem for hanger
Beige-colored florist tape

Fern pins (about 25)
1-pound bunch baby's breath or statice (be sure
to get this amount; bunch sizes vary)

Directions: 1. Unwrap green plastic from straw form and attach hanger. 2. Cover the wreath loosely with larger pieces of baby's breath or statice, using fern pins. 3. Break or cut pieces of baby's breath about 3 inches long. 4. Bundle several pieces together to make a good size bunch. Wrap the wire of the florist pick around the stems. For extra security, a little beige-colored florist tape may be wrapped around the delicate stems and pick, but is not necessary if you work carefully. 5. Insert the picks into the straw form at an angle, working in the same direction. 6. Cover form completely, leaving space for a bow or any other materials you may wish to add. 7. Spray well with hair spray or a clear florist spray to prevent shedding.

NOTE: This wreath serves as the base for most dried flower wreaths.

CAUTION: If you plan to use your wreath year-round, do not hang in a sunny spot; the colors will fade. The humidity of a bath or kitchen will also cause fading. Decorations of dried materials become very brittle in a place that is too hot. Even with good care, they are the least durable of the materials used for Christmas decorations, so handle and store with care!

Favorite Additions: Use other dried materials such as yarrow, dried red and green hot peppers, star flowers, straw flowers, etc. Silk flowers also look especially pretty on a delicate baby's breath base.

HERB AND SPICE WREATH

Directions: 1. Follow directions for "Basic Dried Wreath," using statice, baby's breath, silver king artemisia or rabbit tobacco as a base.* 2. Leave a space in the center for accent herbs. 3. Select herbs with a variety of colors and textures. Good choices are: bay leaves, yarrow, sage, rosemary, lavender, rue, rosehips, lamb's-ears, thyme and oregano. It is easier to work with **fresh herbs,** but remember they shrink when dried so use an extra amount to make the wreath look full. (Although it is more difficult, herbs may be picked in the summer and dried to use in making wreaths later. See directions — "Working with Dried Herbs, Flowers and Grasses.") 4. Attach bundles of herbs to wooden florist picks. 5. Insert picks at an angle and scatter evenly on wreath, working in the same direction. 6. Lay the wreath down flat for herbs to dry; it takes several weeks in a dry, dark place. 7. Spray with hair spray or clear florist spray to prevent shedding.
*A Spanish moss wreath is a quick and easy base for an herb and spice wreath.

Favorite Additions: Small cinnamon bundles tied with bows, bundles of cloves and whole nutmegs tied in nylon hosiery, tiny pomanders made from calamondin oranges or crab apples, net bags of spices or small gingerbread boy cut-outs made from Baker's Clay. Items may be attached with hot glue, florist picks or florist wire.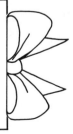

VINE WREATHS

Vines without foliage
Fine gauge florist wire

Select grape vines, if possible, since they make the prettiest wreaths. If they are not available, wisteria, kudzu, honeysuckle or other local vines will do. Cut the vines while still green and pliable. If vines have become dry and stiff, they should be soaked in water for about an hour to make them easier to manage.

Directions: 1. Hold the end of the vine in your left hand. 2. With the right hand make a loop the size you would like the wreath to be. 3. Now, also hold the loop in the left hand along with the end, and continue to make loops with the vine. 4. After 3 or 4 loops, begin to thread the vine in and out around the first loops. 5. Continue until the wreath is the thickness you desire. 6. When a vine runs out, just tuck the end of the vine securely under the other loops of vines. Start another vine in the same manner. 7. If there is any doubt about the vines holding in place, wrap the wreath at intervals with a single piece of fine florist wire. Twist in the back so it will not show. 8. Attach another piece of florist wire or a brown chenille stem to the back of the wreath for a hanger. 9. Attach a bow and/or decorations. Use a hot glue gun to attach decorations. If one is not available, use a clear white glue or attach with wire. If the glued areas show, cover them with Spanish moss.

Favorite Additions: Cones, dried flowers, moss or other dried materials most effectively enhance the natural look of a vine wreath.

MOSS WREATHS —
SPANISH OR PLANTER'S SHEET MOSS

Straw wreath form
Moss to cover wreath
U-shaped fern pins
Chenille stem for hanger
White craft glue or a hot glue gun

Spanish Moss* Directions: 1. Remove green plastic from wreath form. 2. Attach hanger. 3. Pull conditioned moss out in long stringy bunches. Wind moss loosely around wreath form, securing with fern pins as you go. 4. Spray with an inexpensive hair spray. 5. Attach a bow and/or your favorite decorations.

Favorite Additions: A few dried flowers, spaced evenly around the wreath; bird with nest; clusters of pine cones; eucalyptus or sea shells.

Sheet Moss* Directions: 1. Remove green plastic. 2. Attach hanger. 3. With a hot glue gun, glue sheets of moss to the wreath form, fitting the pieces together like a puzzle until the wreath form is covered. If a hot glue gun is not available, U-shaped fern pins may be used to secure the moss after gluing it with a white craft glue.

Favorite Additions: Simple natural decorations — bird and nest, twigs or dried flowers.

*To condition moss, see instructions for "Working with Mosses."

FABRIC WREATHS

BRAIDED WREATH

16-ounce bag of fiberfill
3 6-inch by 42-inch strips of 3 different
but coordinated fabrics
Ribbon or ½ yard of fabric for bow
Plastic cafe curtain ring for hanger

Directions: 1. Fold strips in half, lengthwise, with right sides together. 2. Stitch along edge with ½-inch seam, leaving one end open for stuffing. Turn to right side. 3. Stuff, but not too tightly. Slip-stitch closed. Repeat for other two strips. 4. Tack the 3 strips together at one end. 5. Braid and shape into round wreath. Stitch ends together. 6. Tack a bow onto wreath where the braid has been joined. 7. Sew ring for hanging in back of the wreath. **(If making a fabric bow:** Cut fabric twice as wide as you want bow. Stitch fabric lengthwise with right sides together. Taper ends. Leave an opening to turn inside out. Turn and press flat. Stitch closed. Tie into a bow.)

RUFFLE WREATH

*12-inch styrofoam wreath form with center wire
1 yard of fabric 45 inches wide (includes bow)
2½ yards trim
Plastic cafe curtain ring for hanger

Directions: 1. Cut 2 strips of fabric 12 inches wide and 45 inches long. 2. Join an

end of each to make a strip approximately 12 inches by 90 inches long. Press seam open. 3. Turn under ends and stitch a hem. 4. Fold strips in half, lengthwise, with right sides together and stitch a seam ½-inch from the edge to form a tube with open ends. 5. Press seam open, and turn tube to right side. 6. Stitch length of tube 3½ inches from fold. 7. Add trim to edge with seam. (A ruffle may be stitched into seam when making tube.) 8. Cut through styrofoam **ring and wire** with small saw. 9. Slip tube on wreath form and push to gather. For extra body, the edge with the seam should be the outside ruffle. 10. Glue wreath form back together. Whip tube ends together to finish. 11. Stitch on hanger. 12. Finish with bow of remaining fabric or a ribbon bow.

*Instructions are the same for 10-inch wreath forms. For 14-inch wreath forms, cut 3 strips of fabric 12 inches wide and 45 inches long. (With 1 yard of fabric, there will not be fabric left for a bow.) Other instructions are the same.

BOW WREATH

The variety of choices of ribbon colors and patterns make this a versatile wreath with year-round possibilities. Your choice of ribbons determines the season and the use . . . match a newly decorated bedroom, make a bright colorful spring wreath, or combine red and green patterns for a traditional Christmas wreath.

**12 yards each of three coordinated #9
ribbons (1½ inches wide)
14-inch straw wreath form
50 fern pins
Chenille stem for hanger
Extra ribbon for a bow (optional)**

Directions: 1. Put hanger on wreath. 2. With one of the ribbons make a bow of 5 loops (using "Bow Making" instructions) with each loop measuring 2½ inches (bow will measure 5 inches in diameter). 3. Make two loops; then, make the center loop. This center loop should be the same size as the other 2½-inch loops, **not** smaller as in a regular bow. 4. Now add two more loops and cut end at a slant so that it is the same length as the last loop. 5. Pass fern pin through the center loop and attach to the wreath form. 6. Repeat with other two ribbons. Alternate colors or patterns on wreath form. 7. Cover form with bows in three rows — one on the outside, one on the top and one on the inside. 8. The wreath will be "puffier" if bows are close enough to each other to touch and overlap a little. 9. Add a large bow, if desired.

NOTE: This is not a difficult wreath but is time-consuming. Turn on your favorite T.V. program and "settle in" for about an hour and a half.

NOVELTY WREATHS

Usually these are smaller wreaths — a second wreath or a gift wreath. They start with one of the basic wreaths, but a little imagination and creativity make them an unusual conversation piece and JUST PLAIN FUN.

EDIBLE WREATHS

Edible wreaths . . . a decoration **and** a treat for visiting children!

Cookie Wreaths

Directions: 1. Wrap shaped and decorated cookies individually in clear plastic wrap. 2. Tie them with a yarn or ribbon bow to a permanent green wreath. 3. Decorate the wreath with additional bows of matching ribbon.

Wrapped Candy Wreath

Directions: 1. Tie small cellophane-wrapped candies or plastic-wrapped bundles of candies (such as M & M's) to a permanent green wreath **or** completely cover a straw wreath form with these candies. 2. When covering a wreath entirely with candy, you will work faster by using U-shaped fern pins to attach the candy wrappers or bundles to the wreath form. 3. When candies are tied on a wreath, tie a child's pair of scissors to the wreath with a ribbon long enough to allow for easy snipping.

Gum Drop Wreath

Directions: 1. Break round wooden toothpicks in half. 2. Push the sharp end of the half toothpick into a styrofoam wreath form. 3. Press gumdrop onto broken end. 4. Entirely cover the wreath, leaving room for a bow. For 10-inch wreath form, use about three 9-ounce packages of gum drops.

TOYS, GADGET AND COLLECTIBLE WREATHS

Don't overlook a child's favorite toy, family heirlooms, kitchen gadgets, cookie cutters or an unusual collection as a source of wreath decorations. Search the toy chest, grandmother's attic and flea markets for an interesting addition to your family tradition. Items too large for a tree are often just the right accent for a wreath in your child's room, on the kitchen door or on the back door. Attach these treasured items to one of the basic wreaths with florist wire so they won't be damaged and can be easily removed after Christmas.

PERSONALIZED WREATHS

A personalized wreath is a gift that says, "I made this especially for you" — a cherished decoration and a gift of love. Let your imagination run wild! The ideas are unlimited! These are some favorites:

Occupations:

1. Make a wreath of a cheese crock, complete with a mouse and trap for someone in a **food-related business.** Glue a small block of styrofoam inside the crock. Attach bow, a little permanent greenery, trap and "cheese" to styrofoam. (Cut a yellow sponge into a triangular shape for "cheese.") Hang with a saw-tooth hanger.

2. A **doctor's or nurse's wreath** could contain empty pill bottles and medical items from a child's "doctor kit."

3. A toy telephone on a wreath makes an interesting gift for your club's **telephone chairman.**

4. **Teacher's wreath** has pencils, rulers and, of course, APPLES.

5. There are lots of stuffed bears, both large and small, available at Christmas (not as many "bulls," however). Why not use one to make a wreath for your **favorite stockbroker?**

Hobbies: There are Christmas ornaments available that depict most of the major sports. Use these ornaments on a wreath for your favorite sportsman, or collect small items such as golf tees, tennis balls, fishermen's lures and doll's sporting items at a toy store and design your own. A ship's round life buoy is a perfect wreath for a sailor. A seamstress would enjoy a wreath of small, colorful balls of yarn with knitting needles crossed behind its bow.

"Remember Whens": Dry flowers from a wedding and use them as a gift wreath for the bride's first Christmas. Shells from a trip to the beach or dried flowers from a mountain vacation are reminders of a special time or occasion that was meaningful during the year. Delight your granddaughter with a wreath containing her mother's favorite doll.

Families: Make a yarn doll or gingerbread cookie cut-out to represent each member of the family. Attach them to a wreath. A "family" of gingerbread cookie cutters is available at gourmet shops. Use child's alphabet blocks to spell a family name on a wreath.

Pets: To decorate Fido's dog house, tie small dog biscuits, shaped like bones, to a 10-inch straw form. Use red ribbon or yarn to attach the biscuits. Add a bow of matching ribbon. Don't forget the cat! A favorite cat's wreath might have a catnip toy or a perky Christmas mouse.

BOW MAKING

BASIC SINGLE BOW

For 5-inch diameter bow:
1 18-inch piece florist wire, #22 or #24
1½ yards No. 9 (1½-inch) ribbon
For 10-inch diameter bow:
2 18-inch pieces florist wire, #22 or #24
3 yards No. 40 (3-inch) ribbon
(Instructions for 10-inch bow are shown
in parenthesis.)

A.

Directions: 1. Grasp the ribbon about 2½ (5) inches from one end with the right side of the ribbon facing you and the short end of the ribbon pointing down. 2. Hold ribbon between thumb and forefinger of either hand. 3. With the other hand make a 2½ (5) inch loop upward and away from you. 4. Slip the ribbon between your thumb and finger, gathering the ribbon beside — **not on top of** — the other ribbon. (Diagram A) 5. Make another 2½ (5) inch loop downward and toward you, making sure the right side of the ribbon is on the outside of each loop. (Diagram B) 6. Repeat until 4 loops have been made. Always gather the ribbon with as tiny gathers as possible; this helps the finished bow to "puff." 7. You are now ready for the center loop which gives the bow a professional look and hides the wire. Bring ribbon toward you, up and over, (Diagram C) and around the thumb. (If ribbon has a wrong side, twist ribbon to keep right side on outside.) This loop should be about 2 (4) inches — not quite as long as the others. Gather ribbon between thumb and finger as before. (Diagram D) 8. Make 2 more regular loops — now a total of 7 with center loop — and the bow itself is complete. 9. Wiring the bow to make it hold is a very important part of making a pretty bow. (Bend the florist wire in half first; it will be easier to tighten.) Slip the wire through the center loop, under your thumb. (Diagram E) 10. Bring wire to back of bow and twist securely to hold. 11. Now cut ribbon even with loops. 12. Hold bow tightly at wired area and fluff out loops with your fingers. At this point you have a pretty single bow that many people prefer to the fuller "pom pom" effect. Stop here, or continue to next step for "pom pom" bow.

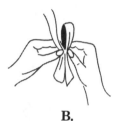

B.

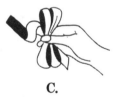

C.

D.

E.

POM POM BOW

Important!!: For a pom pom bow, you will need double the amount of ribbon needed for a "Basic Single Bow," a total of:

6 yards for 10-inch bow
3 yards for 5-inch bow

Directions: Make a second "Basic Single Bow," but eliminate the center loop. Wire this bow behind the first bow at right angles. Twist tightly.

Streamers: To add streamers to either bow, cut an extra piece of ribbon ½ yard long for the 5-inch bow and 1 yard long for the 10-inch bow. Pinch the ribbon a little off-center and secure with the wire holding the bow. On a straw wreath form, just use a fern pin to pin it to the wreath **under** the bow. This makes it easier to detach and press if moisture makes it curl. "Finish" the ends with a slant cut or with an inverted "V."

Words of Wisdom about Bows:
- Most velvet and fabric craft ribbon may be cut lengthwise into varying widths. Acetate ribbons such as taffeta and satin, however, will ravel.
- Once you start making a bow, don't let go or you will have to start over.
- Store your bows carefully each year. Stuff loops with tissue paper and cover with a lightweight plastic or put them in a box.
- AND LAST!! Don't be discouraged if bow-making seems awkward at first. Practice on toilet paper or old ribbon. It will become easier with practice. Six bows and you'll be a pro!

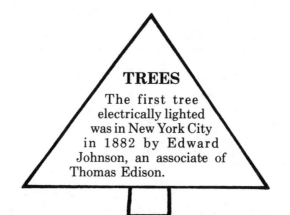

TREES

The first tree electrically lighted was in New York City in 1882 by Edward Johnson, an associate of Thomas Edison.

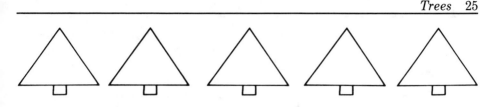

THE CHRISTMAS TREE

This German tradition — the CHRISTMAS TREE — has become America's all-time favorite decoration. Though they may range from a small table tree to the gigantic national tree in Washington, D.C. or be metal, plastic, silk or fresh, no other decoration creates the magic of Christmas like a tree decorated to its owner's special taste. For maximum enjoyment of your tree, follow a few simple rules of selection, care and safety.

SELECTION AND CARE: When buying your tree, test it for freshness. If the needles bend, are resilient and hold when touched, the tree is fresh. Run your hand over the bottom of the cut stump area and, if it is moist and sticky, the tree is still fresh. Bump the cut end on the ground to see if needles shed. As soon as you take the tree home, saw off the trunk about 2 inches above the cut so it can absorb water. Keep it in water until ready to use. For a preservative, either add 1 cup of sugar to each gallon of water or use the following recipe for a more complete preservative that will help preserve color, stimulate moisture absorption and stop bacteria.

Preservative: ¼ cup micronized iron or 4 iron tablets
1 gallon hot water
½ cup light corn syrup or 1 cup sugar
2 tablespoons chlorinated household bleach

After the tree is brought inside, keep the preservative in the base container at all times.

Safety Tips:
1. Keep tree away from heat sources.
2. Check strands of lights and extension cords **before** putting them on tree. Check for loose sockets and frayed wires. Use only UL approved lights.
3. Never use indoor lights outdoors. Cover outdoor plugs and connections that are touching the ground.
4. Keep lights and cords away from the tree's water supply.
5. Use no more than three sets of lights on each extension cord.
6. If you have an artificial plastic tree, use only midget lights designed for these trees. **NOTE:** These midget lights usually push in. Do not twist them!
7. Metal trees should be flood-lighted only.
8. Never leave tree unattended. An 8 foot tree can burn completely in 27 seconds and creates tremendous heat.
9. Never light decorative candles on the tree.

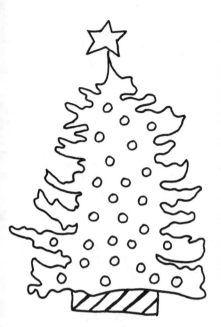

THE LIVING CHRISTMAS TREE: The use of living trees that can later be planted outside or used in a container on the porch or patio increases each year. The success of your living tree will depend upon the care it receives **indoors.** 1. Select one in a container or balled in burlap. 2. First place tree in a heavy plastic bag, then into its container (a produce basket from the grocery store is a good size and can be spray painted). 3. Water the tree just enough to keep it moist. Too much water may encourage new growth which will suffer when moved outside. 4. Place in a cool location in the room and move outside within 2 or 3 weeks. 5. Prepare the hole in advance and line it with straw or other insulation to prevent freezing. Dig the hole at least twice as large as the root ball. 6. Take the tree outside gradually. Keep it in the garage or in a shelter for several days before planting so that it can adjust to the outdoor climate.

TREE LIGHTING FORMULA: Height of tree* times width of tree times 3 equals the number of lights needed. **Formula:** Height X width X 3 = number of lights. When using midget lights multiply number by two. *Measure tree in feet.

Helpful Hint: To change colored lights to white lights, use nail polish remover to remove the color.

HOMEMADE "SNOW": 2 cups Ivory Snow or other white detergent powder
½ cup water
Beat with mixmaster until stiff. "Paint" on the tips of the tree branches. Snow will get hard and stiff.

CREATIVE TREE DECORATIONS: Our favorite decoration is a collection of one-of-a-kind family memorabilia — collected on vacations, made by the children or friends and a few new treasures added each year. If you are just beginning your "collection" or if you enjoy creating a few new ornaments each year, try some of these ideas:

1. String popcorn (stale popcorn is best) and cranberries on heavy polyester thread. Use shorter lengths of thread — about 36 to 45 inches so it will not tangle. Thread a crewel embroidery needle and knot one end, leaving a 4-inch tail beyond the knot. If you are using popcorn, a 10-ounce can of kernels is enough for a 7-foot tree. After you have filled the thread, tie a knot leaving a 4-inch tail on this end, too. Use these "tails" to tie the strings together. String cranberries the same way. It will be easier if you poke the needle through the stem-end first and then through the fresh cranberry. Cranberries are hard so you may need to use a thimble. Sweet gum balls and hemlock cones also make good tree garlands.

2. Tie dried hydrangea blossoms on the tree with a pretty ribbon. Old-fashioned Victorian nosegays (tussie mussies) made with dried flowers or herbs and dried baby's breath may be tucked among the branches. See instructions for drying under "Working with Dried Herbs, Flowers and Grasses" in chapter on "Natural Materials." Complete tree with lots of Queen Anne's Lace snow-flakes.

Queen Anne's Lace Snow Flakes

Pick Queen Anne's Lace in the summer and remove stems. Press the flowers between the pages of a heavy book. Weight the book down, and put it in a warm, dry place for several weeks. Remove flowers and spray with hair spray. Glue a loop of thin gold thread, a ribbon or lightweight fishing line to the back of the flower for hanging. Scatter them on the tree for a delicate finishing touch (the more the better).

---

3. Natural materials such as pine cones, pods, cotton bolls, nuts and sweet gum balls add a Colonial touch. They may be wired on or tied on with bows. An entire tree of cotton bolls tied on with red bows is a Southern favorite. If some cotton is missing, glue packaged cotton balls (from the drugstore) in the empty spaces.
4. Make cookie cut-outs from the recipes for Gingerbread Boys and Sugar Cookies. Make permanent "Gingerbread" cut-outs of brown felt decorated with rick-rack and buttons. They may also be made from sandpaper by cutting two sandpaper gingerbread boys and gluing the wrong sides together. Decorate with yarn and buttons.
5. Collect small toys at flea markets and attic sales. Children also enjoy having their own favorite toys used as tree decorations.
6. Bows, large and small, made of ribbons or fabric (starched heavily and cut with pinking shears) are quick and inexpensive tree decorations.
7. Make homemade fabric ornaments using cookie cutters for patterns. Stitch, stuff and decorate with rick rack, braid and buttons. Add a few herbs or spices to the stuffing for fragrance. To a stuffed gingerbread boy, add the spices you use in gingerbread, etc.
8. Clean out the sewing basket and decorate satin balls with bits of lace, ribbon, beads and sequins.
9. If you are a "collector," use your collectables to decorate a tree — a mouse tree, an angel tree, an owl tree, a pig tree — the possibilities are unlimited.
10. Bells! Bells! Bells! Decorate with small and large bells: sleigh bells, jingle bells, ceramic bells or small cow bells.
11. Make ornaments of Baker's Clay, Bread Clay or Snowflake Frosting (recipes follow).

BAKER'S CLAY* (For ornaments, baskets or larger items)

4 cups flour
1 cup salt
1½ cups water (or less)

Thoroughly mix salt and flour. Gradually add water and mix after each addition. Use a little less than called for and add the extra only if needed. Knead dough on lightly floured surface for 7-10 minutes until smooth and pliable. At this point dough may be stored in a sealed plastic bag in the refrigerator for several days or used immediately. Roll dough out about ¼ " thick; then, use cookie cutters to cut out tree ornaments. Use a nail or a straw to make a hole at the top of each ornament for hanging. Make designs with a toothpick or form small pieces of dough into the shapes you want and moisten with water to attach to ornaments. Use toothpick to push the two dough pieces together. Bake on a cookie sheet at 350° for 30 minutes or longer until fully dry. (Larger items such as wreaths and baskets should be baked at 200° overnight.) When cool, paint or decorate with white glue and glitter. Hang with a ribbon or cord since the salt will rust metal hangers. Recipe makes many ornaments or one basket. In damp climates, softening may be a problem, so seal with several coats of clear lacquer, varnish or acrylic paint. Paint the ornaments or dip them in paint — do not use spray paint because it is not thick enough. Store in tightly sealed plastic bags. Sealing is a **must** with larger items. **NOTE:** Be sure to wash cookie cutters thoroughly because the salt in this recipe is extremely corrosive.
***CAUTION!** NOT TO BE EATEN!

BREAD CLAY* (For detailed ornaments)

8 large pieces old-fashion white bread with crusts removed
8 tablespoons white glue such as Elmer's or Sobo (or less)

Break bread into very small pieces. ("Day old" bread is less expensive and works as well.) Stir in enough glue to form a stiff "clay." Colors may be kneaded directly into dough or painted on later. If mixing colors in the dough, plan to air-dry the ornaments or use colors that will not bake out. Food colors bake out at temperatures over 200°. Dough dries beige in color. If you want white dough, knead white tempera paint into the dough. This is a fine-textured dough, good for small details. It is sturdy and does not soften in humid weather but is more expensive to make. It does not go very far and makes only a few ornaments. Bake at 300° for about 30 minutes or air-dry until hard. Dough keeps several months in the refrigerator in a plastic bag.
NOTE: Insects like these ornaments. Store in a sealed plastic bag with a few moth balls.
***CAUTION!** NOT TO BE EATEN!

SNOWFLAKE FROSTING ORNAMENTS

1 cup confectioners sugar
1 egg white
⅛ teaspoon cream of tartar
¼ teaspoon vanilla

Beat egg white, sugar and cream of tartar until very thick. Beat in vanilla. Spoon frosting into a pastry bag, cake decorator or a plastic bag. If using a plastic bag squeeze frosting into a corner of the bag and cut off a tiny tip of the corner. (The hole's size determines the thickness of the snowflake.) Draw a snowflake design the size you want on a piece of paper with a small, dark, felt-tip pen. Place the pattern under a sheet of waxed paper. Squeeze the frosting onto the waxed paper, following the lines of the design. Let the snowflake harden overnight, then gently remove the waxed paper backing. Attach a loop of dark thread for hanging.

THEME TREES

Wildlife Tree: Decorate a tree growing outside with edible ornaments for the birds and wildlife friends. If you do not have a tree outside, buy one a day or two before Christmas for little cost or decorate your discarded tree for a favorite children's after-Christmas activity. Good edible ornaments: popcorn, marshmallow and cranberry strings; day-old doughnuts tied with ribbons; pine cones with suet; day-old bread figures cut out with cookie cutters; orange baskets made of orange halves and filled with seeds, nut meats, suet, and bits of apples. (To make simple orange baskets: cut orange in half, scoop out pulp, punch 3 holes equal distance around edge, insert pipe cleaners in holes and twist to secure. Hang on tree.) String gum drops on small gauge wire and hang vertically on tree or cover the surface of a small styrofoam ball with gum drops held in place with tooth picks.

Kitchen Tree: Tie smaller items used in the kitchen on a small table tree. Use cookie cutters, bundles of several sticks of cinnamon tied with a bow, cookie ornaments, whole nutmeg wrapped in pieces of nylon hosiery, fabric bags of whole cloves or doll-sized kitchen utensils purchased at toy stores.

Child's Tree: Don't forget that children enjoy having a tree to decorate in their own rooms. Try a toy tree or a paper tree with paper chains, children's art work, or cut-outs from old Christmas cards. A never-fail favorite is a Sugar Plum Tree with edible decorations — candy canes, hard candy, lollipops, cookies, candy kisses and bundles of M and M's tied in clear plastic wrap.

Sea Shell Tree: Make a family project of collecting a variety of shells at the beach. Clean and dry them thoroughly. (To make them whiter they may be left in the sun or cleaned with household bleach.) Drill a small hole in the shells about ¼ inch from the top. For a shiny finish "paint" with several coats of a mixture of ½ white glue and ½ water. Allow to dry thoroughly between coats. Tie on the tree with bows of narrow red ribbon or yarn. Use a star fish for the top of the tree.

Bird Tree: Cover a tree with birds and birds' nests.* Add other decorations that compliment the color of the birds and help carry out the nature theme (such as pinecones and dried flowers). Tie bundles of wheat with small bows. **Bird Seed Balls:** Spray or brush glue on small styrofoam balls and coat with bird seed; insert a piece of wire for hanging. **Nests:** Method 1. Make birds' nests of Spanish moss by winding the moss around your fingers several times to make a nest shape the desired size. Method 2. A sturdier, more permanent nest can be made with excelsior or Spanish moss and glue: Mix flour and water to glue consistency. Soak excelsior thoroughly in glue. Mold nest to fit bird. Place on waxed paper to dry for several days. Eggs may be bought at a Christmas shop or use dried peas for miniature nests. Tuck the nests among the branches.

The long-standing custom of a bird's nest in the Christmas tree had its beginning in German folklore. According to an ancient German legend, those who found a nest in their Christmas tree were certain to have happiness and good fortune the coming year. Add a "good luck" nest (a real one is a treasure) to your tree, and give one to a friend with a note about the legend — wishing her the same happiness and good fortune.

DECORATIONS
"ALL THROUGH THE HOUSE"

Christmas decorating should be a family affair. Begin your celebration by reading the Christmas story together and putting the family nativity scene or créche (the French word for cradle) in its place. Throughout the season make this the focal point of your home. Créches are available in all sizes, styles and prices. If there are small children in the home, be sure it is not breakable. (If necessary, purchase an inexpensive, plastic second one.) The Christmas story becomes more real to children when they are allowed to handle the pieces.

COLONIAL FANS

"Colonial Fans" are fruits and leaves stapled and wired to plywood forms that have been cut to fit over doorways. If you plan your design using local natural materials and simple symmetrical styling, it will reflect Colonial decorating — a reminder of the past when life was simple and hospitality genuine.

> **Plywood, cut to fit over doorway**
> **Tenpenny finishing nails**
> **Wire — lightweight *and* heavy**
> **Screw eyes**
> **Fruit**
> **Large leaves for background**
> **Greenery, pine cones and/or berries**

Directions: 1. Before you start, be sure to condition all materials, using instructions in "Working with Natural Materials." 2. Sketch design on plywood. 3. Staple on leaves for the background or use green thumb tacks. 4. Drive tenpenny finishing nails slanting up into the plywood to hold apples, oranges and smaller fruit. 5. Pineapples and heavy items should be wired to screw eyes in the plywood. 6. To attach berries, pine cones or additional greenery, twist fine florist wire around nails driven into the plywood. 7. Secure fan to window or wall with screw eyes and heavy wire.

DECORATIVE CONTAINERS

Interesting containers for fresh and dried arrangements, gifts, or food are simple to make and are favorite gifts to special friends.

Moss Baskets:

Basket-size plastic container
Planters moss — enough to cover basket
Pliable vines for handle (3-9 pieces) —
grapevines, kudzu, wisteria or honeysuckle
Florist wire
Hot glue gun, white glue or rubber cement

Directions: 1. Select a plastic container such as ones that hold dairy products, ice cream or salads. 2. With a hole punch or ice pick, punch two holes opposite each other and ¾ inches below the rim for the handle. 3. Wrap a piece of fine florist wire around the vines at one end. The number of vines will vary depending on their size. 4. Braid them into a handle that will be about 1½ times the height of the basket. If vines are too stiff, soak them in water for about 30 minutes. They will shrink a little when dry, so allow for this. 5. When the handle is braided, wrap another piece of wire around the other end. 6. Attach each end of the arched handle to the inside of the basket with wires that have been inserted through the two holes. 7. Wrap wires tightly to secure. 8. Put glue on the back of each piece of moss* and cover the outside of the container — fitting the pieces together as you would a puzzle. 9. Moss should extend about an inch over the bottom and top rims. 10. Glue down any loose pieces and glue moss over top and bottom rims.

***NOTE:** If using a hot glue gun, put the glue on the container rather than on the moss.

Grapevine Baskets: Grapevines
Florist wire
Spanish moss

Directions: 1. Select vines that bend easily — ones that are still alive. If green ones are not available, soak dried ones about 30 minutes until they are pliable. 2. Hold end of a vine in one hand. With the other hand, make a loop the diameter of the desired basket. 3. Continue to make loops, weaving the vines under and over each other and upward to make the sides of the basket. When needed, secure with a little florist wire, but it will be prettier if you insert the new vine ends under the other vines. 4. Make a handle like the one for the preceding moss basket and insert the two ends opposite each other into the sides of the basket. Secure handle with wire, glue or very small vines. 5. There is no need for a bottom if you plan to use it for fresh flowers — just set the basket over a clear glass flower container with Oasis. If the basket needs a bottom, however, you may glue on a brown corrugated one or criss-cross larger pieces of vine by sticking them through the bottom vines of the basket. Secure with glue. Trim even with the sides. 6. Cover wire, glue or any "bad spots" with Spanish moss. Fill the basket with additional moss.

Peppermint Candy Cane and Bread Stick Baskets: Follow directions for "Spicy Cinnamon Baskets"* in "The Fragrance of Christmas," but substitute candy canes and bread sticks for cinnamon sticks. (*Page 42)

ARRANGEMENTS

Basic Guidelines:
1. The arrangement's location will determine the size and the type container and materials used. The height of an arrangement should be about 1½ times the height of the container.
2. Select materials with a variety of colors, textures and sizes.
3. The greenery and flowers dictate the type foam needed to securely hold them in place. Use Oasis for fresh flowers and greenery, Designer's Choice for dried materials with delicate stems, and green styrofoam for silk and wired-stem permanent greenery.
4. Secure styrofoam and Designer's Choice in container with florist stickum or secure Oasis with anchoring tape.
5. Cover foam with planter's or Spanish moss.
6. First position tallest top stem and longest side stems to establish basic line and design.
7. Next, add heavier greenery, then larger focal flowers or fruits in odd numbers.
8. Add smaller or secondary flowers with the smallest ones added last.
9. For a natural look, vary lengths of stems.
10. When adding berries, fruit or pine cones without stems, use 3 inch or 6 inch wooden florist picks for securing them in the foam. As with other large accent materials, use an odd number of large fruit pieces.

NOTE: When you need a low, over-sized arrangement and no container is available, ask your florist to sell you a "casket saddle" with Oasis. For low, inexpensive plastic containers that will not show in an arrangement, check discount stores or your kitchen cabinet for plastic food containers that could be sprayed green.

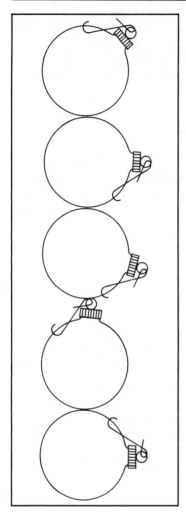

Favorite Arrangements:

● Polished magnolia leaves in a silver bowl mixed with red Christmas balls.

● Lots of fresh greenery and natural materials everywhere!

● Basket of polished red apples with boxwood tucked into crevices. A pretty addition is clusters of long cinnamon sticks — adds fragrance, too.

● A pineapple, the symbol of hospitality, surrounded with fruit and fresh greenery.

● An antique crystal container filled with colorful lollipops, candy canes and hard candies.

● Williamsburg Cones or Trees — These fruit (usually apple) cones may be made on four different type bases. Each uses a different technique for assembling the cone.

Williamsburg Cones

1. **Aluminum Tree:** 1. The easiest base is a purchased **aluminum "tree" or pyramid form** made with large circles that hold the fruit without piercing or bruising it. Place the fruit in the pockets and fill the crevices with boxwood. The fruit is not damaged so may be eaten later. The wire fruit "tree" is pretty year-round; just eliminate the boxwood.

2. **Wooden Cone:** The most often used base is a **wooden cone*** with slanting ten penney finishing nails driven in place to hold the fruit. Drill holes for nails about 1½ inches apart in even circles from bottom to top. Spray cone a dark green and put nails in place. Place a shiny apple on each nail, or on two nails if it turns, and fill the gaps with boxwood. Place polished magnolia leaves around the base and, if desired, affix a pineapple on the top.

*A good size is a cone 12 inches high and 5 inches in diameter at the base. A pineapple on top is more secure if the pointed top has been cut off to leave a flat top about 2 inches in diameter. A hole should be bored in the center of this top to hold a nail for the pineapple.

3. **Styrofoam Cone:** Use a large **12 inch styrofoam cone** instead of a wooden one, but the method of decorating is the same. Use 3 inch wooden florist picks instead of nails to hold the fruit. Insert boxwood right into the cone or put short pieces on wooden picks.*

4. **Cabbage:** Three graduated cabbages were stacked and used by Colonial women as a base for their fruit cones. Slice a silver off the bottom of the largest cabbage for a stable foundation and off the top of the smallest cabbage to hold the pineapple. Force a skewer, a knitting needle or a pointed wooden dowel from top to bottom to hold the cabbages together. Proceed as with styrofoam cone.*

*DANGER!! The dye in some florist picks is poisonous. **Do not eat fruit that has been punctured with a florist pick!**

Extra Large Cones and Arrangements: When making large items with fresh greenery, remember they are heavy. For a cone of fresh greenery, make a chicken wire cone and fill it with sphagnum moss or Oasis. For large arrangements, wrap Oasis in chicken wire and "tie" chicken wire with small pieces of florist wire. Secure in container with heavy Oasis anchoring tape.

GARLANDS

Fresh Greenery Garlands: Tie small bunches of conditioned greenery to a rope that has been died dark green. Use florist wire to wrap the bunches of greenery. Attach them to the rope with all the greenery going in the same direction. Attach ribbon, pine cones or other decorations to the garland with wire.

Extra Large Garlands: For a large, thick, fresh garland, roll under the edges of a strip of chicken wire that is about 6 inches wide and the desired length. Use florist wire to secure pieces of greenery to the "garland."

Permanent Garlands: If you want a garland that can be reused each year, some very pretty ones are available in Christmas shops in many different styles and materials. Commercial garlands are 9 feet long unless otherwise marked. Remember to plan for extra length if you hang your garland with a series of swags. Attach berries, pine cones or other decorations with fine florist wire. A red ribbon laced loosely through the garland and accented with red bows adds color and interest.

CHRISTMAS MAGIC USING WHAT YOU HAVE

- **Baskets and Bowls:** Fill containers with fresh greenery, fruit, pine cones or pods.
- **Bows:** Tie bows on pillows, chandeliers, candlesticks, lampposts, mailboxes, pets, and fireside brooms.
- **Old Toys:** Recycle old toys — arrange them under the tree or in a child's wagon.
- **Family Treasures:** Decorate with your cherished antiques and collectibles — an important part of your Christmas tradition. "Dress" a collection of animals for the holidays.
- **Bird Feeders:** Glue artificial red bird in feeder. Attach greenery and a bow.
- **Yule Log:** Select the largest or most interesting log in the woodpile. Tie it with a bow, add greenery and save it beside the fire for Christmas Eve.
- **Hurricane Globes:** Fill globes with Christmas balls or apples. Scatter greenery in the niches.
- **Folding Hat Racks:** Hang ornaments or colorful balls from an antique folding hat rack. Tie a bow on the end of each knob.
- **Family Scrapbook:** Take the family scrapbook out of the closet and put it on the coffee table. Christmas is a time to relive happy memories and to add new ones to your "collection."
- **Duck Decoy:** Surround a favorite duck decoy with polished magnolia leaves and pieces of fresh fruit.

BASIC TREE SKIRT

45-inch fabric circle — quilted, plain or felt
Braid, trim or decorations of your choice

Directions: 1. Before cutting fabric, make a newspaper or brown paper pattern. 2. Most tree skirts are a circle 45″ in diameter, but if you have a tree that is 7 feet or taller, you might want a larger skirt. Either buy wider fabric or sew two pieces together before cutting the circle. The seam should be in the center. 3. Mark the center of the circle and cut a straight line from the edge to the center point. If you are using two pieces of fabric, open the seam to the center. 4. Cut a 4-inch diameter circle in the center for the tree trunk. Hem or bind the two straight sides cut into the center. 6. Bind edges of small center circle with bias tape. 7. The edging of the larger outer circle should be incorporated in your overall design. 8. Decorate and trim skirt to coordinate with the theme of your tree or the decor of your home.

Favorite Tree Skirts: Cross-stitch fabric decorated with Christmas cross-stitch designs — Quilted fabric with drapery fringe on the edge — Felt skirt with scalloped edge and felt cut-outs (patterns may be found in children's coloring books) — Patchwork or calico skirt with "country" rickrack and eyelet ruffles — A "family" skirt with a figure to represent each family member — A skirt of a solid color, stenciled with your favorite design. (Cut stencil design from lightweight cardboard and paint with a fabric paint.)

BASIC FABRIC STOCKING

2 pieces of fabric 12 X 22-inches (quilted or plain)
6-inches of grosgrain ribbon or bias tape to match fabric

Directions: 1. Enlarge pattern on paper (see "Enlarging a Pattern"). 2. The pattern is the **actual size of the finished stocking,** so allow 1-inch seams on the sides and bottom and 2 inches at the top for a hem. 3. Decorate and trim the stocking pieces either before or after cutting it out, but **before** stitching it together. 4. Cut out 2 pieces, making sure the front and back are cut in opposite directions. 5. Pin right sides together. 6. Stitch together with a 1-inch seam. 7. Trim seam to ½ inch and clip curved edges. 8. Press seams open. 9. Turn down 2 inches at the top; then, turn raw edge under ½ inch. 10. Stitch or whip to finish hem. 11. Turn stocking to right side. 12. Fold ribbon or tape in half and stitch securely inside the back corner of stocking. **For A Cuff:** For a cuff on the stocking, allow 4 inches at the top when cutting the stocking. Make a 4 inch hem then fold back a 2 inch cuff. Tack to secure. **Easy Felt Stocking:** 1. Use same pattern for fabric stocking but cut out finished size with no seam allowance. 2. Sew decorations and trim on stocking pieces. Although felt stocking trim may be glued, sewing is recommended because it makes the stocking more durable and neater. It is worth the extra time and effort. If you are in a hurry, however, and want to use glue, wait until the stocking is completed to attach the trim. 3. Pin wrong sides of pieces together, being careful that edges match. 4. Fold ribbon in half. Insert and pin ends in back corner of stocking to make hanging loop. 5. Topstitch around sides and bottom ¼ inch from edge, stitching over the ribbon loop several times.

1 square = 1 inch

NOTE: For a different look, cut out felt stocking with pinking shears.

Favorite Stocking Creations: Felt stocking with Christmas cut-outs sewed on and trimmed with beads and sequins. Cut name out in felt letters — Quilted stocking (quilt your own) — A "crazy quilt" stocking with velvet patches — Solid-colored fabric stocking with a different applique for each family member. Use Christmas cut-outs or be creative with hobbies or special interests — Victorian satin or velvet stocking trimmed with antique lace or doily — Needlepoint, cross-stitch and embroidery stockings — "Clean the Sewing Box" stocking with an artistic design of lace, rickrack and braid — Corduroy stocking for the man in the family — Country muslin stocking with a stencil design. Cut design from lightweight cardboard and paint with fabric paint. Stenciling on felt may be done with spray acrylic paint — Calico stocking with a coordinated solid color for the cuff. Embroider name on the cuff — Smaller stockings for family pets. Tie on dog milk bones with red yarn pieces that have been sewn on the stocking (or make a small felt stocking the shape of a dog bone) — Extra large stocking for an extra special person — Stocking in college colors for a college student.

ENLARGING A PATTERN

Many patterns in Christmas and craft books are drawn on graphs of small squares. To enlarge these patterns you need to draw a larger graph on paper large enough to accommodate the size squares indicated on the pattern. Example: if pattern says "one square equals 1 inch", then draw your squares 1 inch in size. If you do not want to draw your own squares, large graph paper may be bought at fabric, art or office supply stores. Since it is available in many sizes, be sure to get the proper size squares.

First, mark off the correct number of squares both horizontally and vertically. Writing in the margin, number the rows on the original pattern and do the same on corresponding rows of the larger graph.

Starting at the top, left-hand square move across the larger graph marking each square to correspond with the same square on the original. With a pencil, put dots on the lines of each square where the design line crosses it. Mark one square at a time. Connect dots after marking a few squares. Be careful to copy the design on the original squares in its corresponding square as closely as possible.

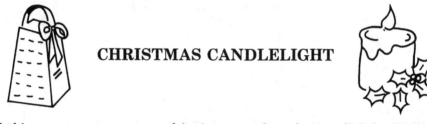

CHRISTMAS CANDLELIGHT

Nothing creates a more cozy and festive atmosphere than candlelight. Use lots of candles everywhere, and for variety, use different groupings of candleholders. Tie ribbons around the base of the candleholders. In addition to the traditional brass, wooden, glass and silver candlesticks, try some creative ideas. Use votive candles in muffin tins, tart pans, cheese graters or small clay flower pots. Almost anything will become a candle holder by using simple metal or plastic holders with picks which are available at florists or trim-a-tree shops. Insert these candle holders in wreath forms, in styrofoam or even in fruit. An apple makes an excellent country candle holder. Insert the candle holder with pick and add a small bow. **CAU-TION‼** Remember to keep the flame away from **anything** that will burn!

YULE LOG CANDLEHOLDER:
   Small log, cut the length desired
   Tapers
   Natural greenery

Directions: 1. Select a log cut neatly at the ends and one that will sit steadily on a flat surface. 2. Drill holes ⅞ inches in diameter and 1½ inches deep in log to hold candles. 3. Decorate with natural greenery.

LUMINARIES (OUTDOOR PAPER BAG LANTERNS): Wonderful outdoor lighting! Line walks with these inexpensive lanterns.
   Brown paper bags (approximately lunch bag size), 5½ x 10⅝ x 3⅛ inches or a little larger
   Votive candles
   Sand

Directions: 1. If you wish to decorate the bags, do this first. Your children will delight in painting designs on the bags. An interesting design of holes may be made by punching holes in the bag with a hole punch. Try a snowflake design. Check party stores for colored bags. 2. Roll top of bag down until it is about 8 inches tall. This makes bag stronger so it will not blow into flames. 3. Pour in about 2 or 3 cups of sand until bag is ¼ full. 4. Place votive candle in center of sand and light. 5. **CAUTION!** Do not put luminaries near leaves. 6. Larger bags may be used, but use enough sand so they will not blow over.

FAVORITE CANDLE TIPS:
1. Candles burning at a party help to cut down on smoke in the room.
2. Put candles in the freezer several hours before using. This will help to reduce dripping, and they will burn more slowly.
3. Save candle stubs to melt later and make new candles.
4. Place candles (votive candles or crystal candleholders are especially pretty) on mirrors for a breathtaking reflection. Purchase an antique beveled mirror at a flea market or have a mirror cut to size by a glass company. Be sure to have the edges smoothed.

NEW CANDLES FROM OLD CANDLES:

Directions: 1. Melt old candles in an **old** pot **just until they melt.** Remove from stove immediately! **CAUTION!** Once the candles melt, the paraffin gets very hot very quickly. Bits of children's crayons may be added for color. 2. Save the longest candle to use as the candlewick (or wicks may be purchased at craft stores). 3. Cut the top off a wax-coated quart-size milk carton. Place in a large deep pan to catch drippings and as a precaution in case it leaks. 4. With a fork, carefully remove old wicks from the melted paraffin. 5. Hold the wick candle in the center of the milk carton and pour melted paraffin around it until it stands alone. Fill carton to desired height. 6. Leave to harden 24 hours, and tear off carton.

For Ice Candles ("Swiss-Cheese" Candles): Use a ½ gallon milk carton and fill around wick candle with crushed ice (pieces should be ½-1 inch in diameter), then add the hot paraffin.

THE FRAGRANCE OF CHRISTMAS

CHRISTMAS BOIL: To fill the house with the aroma of Christmas spices, brew a spicy mixture on the stove.

2 cups of water
1 tablespoon whole cloves
3 cinnamon sticks
1 whole nutmeg (or 1 teaspoon ground nutmeg)

Directions: Simmer all ingredients in a medium size pan. Add additional water and spices when needed.

POMANDER BALLS: Pomander balls are long-lasting, spicy ornaments made of clove-studded oranges, apples or lemons. They may be hung on the tree, displayed in a pretty bowl or basket or used as a sachet in a closet.

1 thin-skinned orange
1 box whole cloves
1 tablespoon powdered orris root*
1 tablespoon ground cinnamon
1 teaspoon ground nutmeg (optional)
1 teaspoon ground allspice (optional)

Directions: 1. Wash and dry fruit. 2. Use a nail to pierce holes over entire surface of fruit. 3. Press the stem-end of a whole clove into each hole. If ribbon is to be added, leave ribbon-width bands with no cloves. 4. Mix spices in bowl and roll fruit in spices to thoroughly cover. 5. Wrap in tissue paper and allow to dry in dry, airy place for 3-6 weeks until it feels light when picked up. For more even drying, turn fruit every few days. 6. For a finishing touch, tie with ribbon. If it is to be hung or attached to a wreath, either use ribbon or insert a florist wire through entire orange **before** adding cloves and drying. For fruit used in a bowl, add extra interest, punch a hole through the fruit with a fruit peeler and insert a long cinnamon stick before drying. 7. After a few years the fragrance may begin to wane. It can be renewed by washing the pomander in warm water or warming it in a slightly warm oven for about 15 minutes. Sprinkle with a few drops of oil of cinnamon or cloves. Roll in fresh spices.
*Orris root is available in most drug stores or health food stores.

POTPOURRI: Potpourri is a mixture of dried flower petals, herbs, leaves, and spices that create the fragrance of Christmas in every room. In early America potpourri was used year-round as an air freshener. Colonial women created their own mixtures to add charm, a decorative touch and seasonal fragrance to their homes.

1 quart of dried flower petals (such as roses, pansies, larkspur,
   delphiniums, daisies, camellias and/or whole violets)
1½ tablespoons powdered orris root (see pomander balls)
1 teaspoon each: ground cloves, nutmeg, allspice and cinnamon

Directions: 1. Pick flowers early in the morning and use those that are fully opened. To dry, spread on screen in a dry, dark, well-ventilated place. It takes about 3-5 days. 2. Mix dried petals with orris root, nutmeg, cloves and allspice. Only the orris root is a must. Other herbs, spices and oils may be used, so experiment to develop your own special fragrance. Crushed mint, rose-geranium leaves and dried orange peel are interesting fragrances. 3. Store mixture in an air tight jar for several months or use immediately. 4. Use in open bowls and baskets or use to fill sachets.

NOTE: For extra fragrance, after drying but **before mixing,** seal flower petals in a quart jar with 2 tablespoons salt. Leave in a dark place for 3 weeks; then mix as directed.

FIRESIDE FRAGRANCE: Tie and decorate a bundle of 12-inch long cinnamon sticks. Place it on the hearth in front of an open fire. Each time it gets warm, the aroma of cinnamon will fill the room.

KITCHEN SPICE ROPE: Select yarn and fabric colors to match kitchen or use Christmas colors.

> 6 **pieces of yarn, 1 yard long**
> 1 **small plastic curtain ring (about ¾ inch in diameter)**
> 4 **circles of fabric (4 inches in diameter)**
> 1 **tablespoon each: whole cloves, crushed cinnamon sticks, whole nutmeg, dried lemon peel (or select your own spices)**

Directions: 1. Pull the yarn pieces halfway through the plastic ring until each side measures 18 inches. Plait the 12 pieces, using 4 pieces of yarn in each braid. Tie off with another small piece of matching yarn. Leave about 1½ inches unplaited at the end for tassel. 2. Cut fabric circles with pinking shears. Make little bags of spices by putting a tablespoon of a spice in the center of each fabric circle. Tie with matching yarn. 3. Handstitch bags evenly along rope or attach with additional yarn. 4. Hang in the kitchen.

SPICE ORNAMENTS: When making stuffed fabric ornaments, roll polyester batting in mixture of spices before stuffing ornaments. Example: Use ginger, cinnamon, nutmeg and cloves for gingerbread boy or peppermint oil for candy cane. Cookie cutters make good patterns.

HERB AND SPICE WREATHS: See directions under **WREATHS AND BOWS.**

FRAGRANT HOT PADS:

> **2 pieces fabric 9 X 6½ inches**
> **2 pieces quilt batting 8½ X 6 inches**
> **¼ cup herbs or spices with blending fragrances**

Directions: 1. Put right sides of the fabric pieces together; stitch ½ inch from edges, leaving one side open. 2. Trim corners. 3. Turn to right side. 4. Insert 2 pieces of batting and put spices between batting layers. 5. Turn under edges of open side and baste. 6. Stitch around hot pad about ½ inch from edge to secure batting. 7. Shake to distribute spices evenly. Hot pad gives off scent of herbs and spices when a hot dish is placed on it. Make a variety of sizes to fit different dishes.

SPICY CINNAMON BASKETS:

Cinnamon sticks — enough to cover container
*Container desired size
Hot glue gun or quick drying glue
Ribbon

Directions: 1. Select cinnamon sticks a little longer than the height of container. Short ones for tiny "baskets" are available at the grocery store but buy longer ones at craft or trim-a-tree shops where they are less expensive. They may be broken or sawed to fit. 2. Glue cinnamon sticks to container. Use a hot glue gun if one is available. 3. Put a rubber band around cinnamon to secure. (If glue is not quick-drying, put rubber band on container; then, apply glue to cinnamon sticks and stick them **under** the rubber band.) 4. When dry, wrap a ribbon over the rubber band and tie a bow. 5. Line with Spanish Moss or excelsior or use as is. 6. Fill with nuts, candies, greenery or potpourri.
*Small cardboard boxes or containers, mushroom baskets, custard or ice cream cups, and plastic food containers with straight sides make good "baskets."

BALSAM STUFFED PILLOWS: Make a small pillow about 5 to 6 inches square. "Stuff" it with the needles from a balsam tree. This is a good after-Christmas project. Strip needles from your discarded Christmas tree and make pillows for **next** Christmas. Balsam oil may be purchased to restore the fragrance if it fades with age.

Entertaining

Decorating done — now share the warmth of your home with family and friends. Your parties will become an important part of your family's Christmas traditions. Adapt your personal preference for entertaining to your home, your facilities and your budget. Whatever the style of the party, however, it should be fun, sincere and relaxed. **The food, the decorations and the orderliness of the house should take second place to the pleasure of your guests and the joy of being with friends.** The "secret ingredient" to any successful entertaining is a warm, cordial hostess who sincerely enjoys having guests and makes each one feel special. If you have this "secret ingredient," the rest can be learned with advanced planning, organization, attention to details, lots of lists and a little experience.

THE ART OF ENTERTAINING
(Action Plan)

1. Plan ahead! Make your guest list and decide on the menu. **Write them down** — in fact, write everything down.
2. Be specific in your invitations about time, dress, occasion and extent of food.
3. Make arrangements early for extra help if you are having a large group.
4. Plan for table decorations and flowers.
5. Check serving dishes and decide which to use for each dish. Plan where to put them on the table.
6. Clean house, polish silver and set table as far ahead as your family's activities and lifestyle will allow. Have plenty of ashtrays in each room.
7. Make a complete grocery list and finish grocery shopping several days ahead. Remember to include seasonings, garnishes, cocktail napkins, wine, drink mixes, and soft drinks and juices for non-drinkers.
8. Several days before, prepare all dishes that can be made in advance (prepare frozen dishes even earlier). The more you prepare ahead, the more gracious you will seem as a hostess.
9. Determine the location of the bar. Put bar and wine paraphernalia in an out-of-the-way place several days ahead. Be sure to have enough extra ice.
10. Day of the party: Fix flowers; finish last minute food preparations and table setting; check bathrooms for soap, extra toilet tissue and clean towels; then, have a quiet hour to relax before you dress to greet your first guest.

FAVORITE HINTS FOR
A HAPPIER HOSTESS

- Paint a picture with food. When preparing your menu, remember to vary color and texture of food. Food should be pretty as well as good. Garnishes should not be just an "afterthought" but should be included in your plans for each dish.

- Include in the menu as many dishes as possible that can be frozen or prepared a day or two ahead of time. Try to include a variety of flavors and temperatures of both raw and cooked foods.

- Plan generously for your guests and freeze leftovers for your family. A skimpy table is unattractive, and running out of food is embarrassing.

- Any party is more enjoyable if you have sufficient help. It may be a maid, bartender, family member, or your best friend. Be sure, however, they know their duties ahead of time and arrive on time. At a small party, male guests enjoy manning the bar themselves.

- Music adds a festive air, especially at Christmas. Engage a musician to play the piano, guitar, banjo, or violin. If your budget or space is limited, play tapes or records.

- If you are planning a large party with out-of-town guests or a number of people who do not know each other, ask a friend or two to help you see that they are properly introduced.

- "Cocktail Hour" before a meal should never exceed an hour and a half. Guests will be more inclined to appreciate the flavor of the food and to enjoy a more leisurely meal.

- Keep the party moving. Serve the first course in a mug before guests come to the table, plan one course in an unusual place or have the dessert and coffee table in another room. Even at a cocktail party, scatter a few small food trays in rooms other than the dining room.

- The kitchen is great for an informal party. Guests enjoy helping with the preparations, such as "make your own" crepe, omelet, pizza or sundae.

- Keep trays and serving containers replenished so they look full at all times. Keeping an alternate tray in the kitchen for a quick exchange is a simple solution.

- Believe it or not, you'll be a happier hostess the morning after if you clean up the night before.

Hostess Record
When:
What:
Guest List:

Menu:

Notes:

Hostess Record
When:
What:
Guest List:

Menu:

Notes:

The Cocktail Party:
- Keep the number of guests to a comfortable size for your home. If the number becomes too unwieldy, stagger the times on the invitations or try having two parties, two nights in a row.
- Provide small plates for food to allow guests to help themselves and to make moving about easier.
- Invite guests of different ages with a variety of interests. This adds zest and stimulates conversation.
- For more than 35 guests, have two bars.

The Buffet:
- Buffet meals are more enjoyable for everyone if each guest has his own tray — start a collection.

Seated Entertaining:
- To promote conversation, keep the centerpiece low so guests will be able to see across the table.
- Plan the seating arrangement in advance (use place cards if you have trouble remembering). Seat the female guest of honor on the host's right, then alternate men and women around the table.
- Chill plates or bowls for salad and warm plates for the hot entreé.

PARTY NOTEBOOK

Keep a party notebook for later reference. Include important facts such as date, occasion, guest list, menu (with location of recipes), successes and mistakes. Note blue-ribbon favorite foods that disappeared first as well as items that were overbought.

Be a thoughtful hostess and take the extra time to also record any special likes, dislikes or even allergies of specific guests. Don't trust your memory — even the best memory will sometimes fail in the hustle and bustle of busy times.

ICY TIPS FOR PARTY BEVERAGES

● Fill ice trays with punch — when it melts, it won't taste watery.
● Freeze punch in a Christmas mold with strawberries, cherries or blueberries to add color, or put punch and fruit in individual molds and freeze.
● Freeze diluted orange juice or cranberry juice for colorful, flavorful ice.
● Muffin tins make large ice cubes that last a long time.

WINE HINTS

1. White wines should be stored in the ice box prior to serving and served **chilled.** Cold tap water may be used to chill quickly.
2. Red wines should be served at room temperature.
3. Claret, Burgundy and Chianti should be uncorked and placed in the room in which they are to be served for several hours before serving.
4. As cork is being removed, hold the bottle with a napkin in case the neck of the bottle should break. Wipe the rim of the bottle carefully before pouring the first glass.
5. When opening one of the sparkling wine bottles, hold at a 45° angle. Do not let cork fly across the room.
6. Glasses should never be filled more than ⅔ full.
7. Champagne is a dessert wine, but may be served with any course and at all times during the meal.
8. Never follow a sweet wine with a dry wine.
9. Wine should be pleasing to the eye as well as the palate.
10. Any good, simple wine may be served throughout the meal. This is a very practical rule to remember.

WINE CHART

WINE	COURSE
APPETIZER WINES: (White wines only) Dry French wines: Loire Valley Bordeaux (Graves) Chablis, Burgundy Dry German Wine California: Chablis, Chardonnay, Sauvignon Blanc Dry Sherry Champagne	Serve chilled without food or with hors d'oeuvres, nuts and cheeses
SOUP WINES: (Same as above dry wines)	Serve chilled with soup
WHITE DINNER WINES: (Dry wines preferable) Chardonnay (French or California) Sauvignon Blanc Dry Graves or Bordeaux Chablis, Sauterne	Serve chilled with lighter dishes: veal, chicken, fish, lamb, shellfish, omelettes, any white meats, or cheese dishes.

WINE	COURSE
RED DINNER WINES: Pinot Noir Burgundy Claret Zinfindel Beaugolais Rose (chilled) Chianti	Serve at room temperature with hearty red meat dishes: steaks, roasts, chops, large game, cheese dishes, chicken, spaghetti, and other Italian dishes.
DESSERT WINES: Sauterne Sweet Rhine Mosel	Serve chilled or at room temperature with: fruits, nuts, cookies, cheeses, cakes and desserts.
SPARKLING WINES: Champagne Sparkling Burgundy	Serve chilled with any food: appetizers, main course or dessert. (Especially good in party punches.)
AFTER DINNER: Port, Madeira, Cream Sherry, Brandy, Cognac, Liquers, Muscatel	Serve at room temperature, unless frapped.

"PAINTING THE PICTURE" — WITH PARTY FOOD

Your party table should reflect your personal taste so don't be afraid to experiment. Here are some ideas to stimulate your creativity and imagination.

CUCUMBER FISH: On an oblong platter arrange 3 or 4 layers of cucumber rounds in the shape of a fish. Overlap the cumumber slices to resemble fish scales. Use an olive slice for the eye. Cut some of the cucumber rounds in half or in small strips and "fan out" for the tail and fins. Serve with a seafood dip in a large sea shell. This is also a good way to decorate a molded seafood mousse. Garnish with lemon wedges and parsley.

ALMOND CHICKEN: Follow method used for fish to arrange sliced almonds like "feathers" on a molded chicken paté.

PINECONES: Shape a cheese ball to resemble a pinecone. Use whole almonds arranged in layers for scales.

SNOWPEAS SUNBURST: Arrange crisp, whole snowpeas on a round plate in a sunburst pattern. Place dip bowl in center.

YUM YUM WREATH

About 50 fern pins (U-shaped florist pins)
14-inch green styrofoam wreath
3 bunches curly endive or spinach,
washed and chilled
1 small box round toothpicks
2 cucumbers
1 head cauliflower
36 cocktail tomatoes
3 carrots
12 radishes
1 pound shrimp, boiled and cleaned

Attach curly endive to a green styrofoam ring with U-shaped fern pins. Place wreath on a large clear glass platter.* Decorate with clusters of dippables, such as cucumber rounds, cauliflower flowerets, cocktail tomatoes, and shrimp. Attach vegetables with toothpicks to the wreath. Affix a simple red bow to the base of the wreath. Complete decorating with carrot curls and radish roses. Have tooth picks and dip nearby. **NOTE:** It is best to make the bow and the wreath base ahead on the morning of the party and to prepare the vegetables and shrimp ready to serve. Refrigerate and assemble just before guests arrive.
*If a platter is not available, cut a piece of green cardboard to wreath size and cover with clear plastic wrap.

SHRIMP TREE

12 inch or 18 inch styrofoam cone
About 50 fern pins (U-shaped florist pins)
2-3 bunches curly endive
1½-2 pounds shrimp, cooked and cleaned
1 small box round toothpicks
Small red bow for tree top
Florist stickum

Cover styrofoam cone with curly endive that has been washed and chilled. Attach with fern pins — U-shaped florist pins. Starting at the base of the tree, working up, overlap leaves to cover the cone. Refrigerate. When ready to serve, attach shrimp with toothpicks on the tree in a festive pattern. Top with a red pom pom bow that has been wired to a fern pin or toothpick. Place on a large serving platter. If necessary, use florist stickum to secure cone in place. Pile additional shrimp at the base of the tree.

Favorite Variation: Use dipping vegetables on tree instead of shrimp.

BOUNTIFUL HARVEST CENTERPIECE: Mound fresh fruits (to be eaten) and/or vegetables on a long mirror in the center of the table. Use tallest pieces in the center and taper sides with graduated pieces. Smallest pieces should be at the ends. The pineapple, a symbol of hospitality since colonial days, is large enough to be a perfect center focal point. Pineapple boats or scalloped, small melon halves nestled in the arrangement, serve as good flower containers with a plastic liner and floral foam. Small potted plants may be added to the fruits and vegetables. Use bell pepper halves and artichokes as votive candle holders (see page 49) or purchase metal candle holders with picks to stick into apples or oranges.

Favorite Variations: Soup's On: Combine vegetables with flowers in a soup tureen for an informal soup meal. Informal Baskets: Use a large basket or a grouping of smaller baskets to hold some of the flowers, fruits and vegetables. As part of the table decorations have colorful napkins arranged in a matching or coordinating basket.

CONTAINERS:

ASPARAGUS, BREAD STICK, CANDY CANE AND CINNAMON "BASKETS": For directions see index, "Spicy Cinnamon Baskets," in "Decorations All Around the House." Instructions are the same for bread stick, candy cane or cinnamon "baskets." Asparagus baskets are assembled in the same manner, but the spears need to be kept in ice water until a day or two before the party. Dip the cut ends of the asparagus spears in paraffin to seal in the moisture before making the basket. Keep basket refrigerated until time to use. Use as containers for flowers or sauces, dips and other food.

CABBAGE SERVING BOWL: Place cabbage on cutting board, stem end down. Draw an imaginary square on cabbage about ⅓ of the way down the head. With a long, sharp knife, cut along sides of "square", slanting the knife diagonally toward the center. Remove center plug, and use the cut-out center as a dip container. (If you put a small clear glass bowl in the center, refilling will be easier.) Pull off some of the outside leaves, and lay them on the platter around the cabbage. Fill leaves with raw dipping vegetables.

CITRUS BASKETS: Select unblemished lemons, grapefruit or oranges. Cut a very thin slice from the bottoms, if necessary, so they will stand upright. Clean out pulp with a grapefruit spoon. These can be made ahead and frozen. Thaw 10 minutes before using. They are pretty garnishes when filled with cranberries or condiments. Mashed sweet potatoes may be baked in orange shells, salads congealed in grapefruit shells or tartar sauce served in lemon cups.

MELON SERVERS: Cut melons in half. Zig-zag or scallop the top rim. Use melon ball scoop to remove fruit. Leave a ½-inch shell and scrape to even inside surface. Use to hold fruit or as flower containers. Smaller melon halves such as cantaloupe and honeydew may be used as servers or to hold individual servings of chicken or fruit salad. Cut a thin slice from the bottom of the melon halves if they do not sit upright.

PINEAPPLE BOAT: Wash pineapple. With a sharp knife, cut pineapple lengthwise, slicing off about ¼ of the side of the pineapple. Take care to leave the top leaves. Use a paring knife or grapefruit knife to remove the fruit from both sections. Sides should be left about ½-inch thick. Discard the smaller portion and use larger shell as a container for the pineapple chunks, melon balls and a mixture of other bite-size fresh fruit. These "boats" also make excellent flower containers with a plastic liner and floral foam.

SQUASH, CUCUMBER OR BELL PEPPER SHELLS: Squash varieties, cucumbers or bell peppers may all be cut and hollowed out to use as flower containers with florist foam, as servers for dip, or as garnishes when filled with condiments. ments.

PUMPERNICKLE ROUND: Cut top off a round loaf of pumpernickel bread with a serrated knife. Pull out the soft center of the bread. Break into cubes and save for dipping. (Be careful to keep the crust intact.) Fill center with a favorite dip.

ARTICHOKE VOTIVE: Cut the stem off the bottom of the artichoke, so it will stand upright. Slice off the tough top leaves with a knife and trim the tips of the other leaves with scissors. Open the leaves and scoop out the choke with a grapefruit spoon. Place a votive candle in the cavity. Bell peppers also make good votive candle holders!

FAVORITE GLAMOROUS GARNISHES

Frosted grapes — Divide grape bunch into small clusters. Dip each cluster into creme de menthe (or a slightly beaten egg white). Dust generously with confectioners sugar. Freeze 20 minutes, then refrigerate. When ready to serve, sprinkle with more confectioners sugar.

Peach half — Top with ½ teaspoon melted butter, mixed with 1 teaspoon brown sugar. Add 1 teaspoon chutney and broil at 450° until topping bubbles.

Cranberry jelly cut-outs — Slice cranberry jelly ¼ inch thick and cut shapes with cookie cutters. Place on orange slices.

Small skewers with fruit — Sprinkle with brown sugar and curry and broil a few minutes until hot.

Apple wedges — Dip in lemonade concentrate.

Tomato roses — Peel around tomato in a continuous spiral strip about 1-inch wide. (Take care not to break strip.) Curl peel around to resemble a rose.

Lemon or orange wedges and twists
Pineapple spears
Crab apples or brandied peaches
Parsley and watercress
Stuffed mushroom caps
Filled artichoke bottoms
Tomato and onion "cups"
Chopped chives
Carrot curls
Radish roses
Olives
Pimento strips

Broccoli flowerets
Paprika
"Piped" mashed potatoes
Toast points
Pastry cut-outs
Croutons
Hard-boiled eggs — sliced and grated
Slivered nuts
Chocolate curls
Dollop of sour cream
Whipping cream
Mint sprigs

GOLDEN RULE OF GARNISHING: Garnishes should always **harmonize** with the type and taste of the food they are accenting!! They are usually most effective, however, when they contrast in color and texture. Plan them when you plan your menu — perfect garnishes are rarely an accident.

PARTY PORTIONS

Coffee:	1 pound plus 2 gallons of water makes 40 cups.
Punch:	1 gallon of punch fills 40 punch cups. The average guest will have 3+ cups of punch.
Wine:	1 bottle of wine serves 6 four-ounce wine glasses.
Liquor:	1 fifth = 16 (1½-ounce) jiggers
	1 quart = 20 (1½-ounce) jiggers
	A jigger = 1½-ounces (average drink)
	The average guest will have 2+ drinks.
Food:	For cocktail food, count a total of 10 "bites" per person.
Meat:	For Main Dish:
	½ pound shrimp per person
	¼-½ pound beef per person
	¼ pound boneless ham or fish per person
	¼ pound baked poultry per person or 2 pieces fried chicken
	per person
Cheese:	3 pounds of cheese serves 25-30 generously.
Vegetables:	½ cup per person

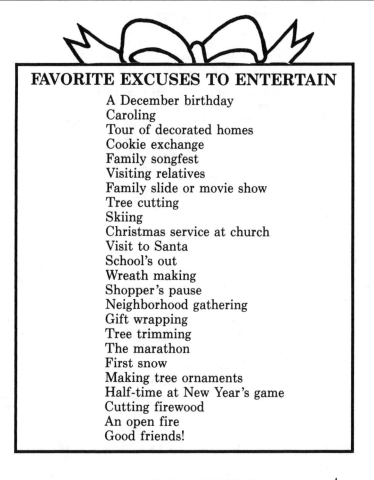

FAVORITE EXCUSES TO ENTERTAIN

A December birthday
Caroling
Tour of decorated homes
Cookie exchange
Family songfest
Visiting relatives
Family slide or movie show
Tree cutting
Skiing
Christmas service at church
Visit to Santa
School's out
Wreath making
Shopper's pause
Neighborhood gathering
Gift wrapping
Tree trimming
The marathon
First snow
Making tree ornaments
Half-time at New Year's game
Cutting firewood
An open fire
Good friends!

PARTIES

COOKIE EXCHANGE

Choose a late morning or mid-afternoon time to invite a dozen or more friends to bring a dozen of their favorite Christmas cookies to exchange. After refreshments and time to visit, provide each guest with a colorful bag to fill with cookies from the other guests' favorites. Each guest takes home a dozen cookies, different from the ones she brought. Good cooks will also appreciate having the cookie recipes included.

Lemon Apples*   Sugared Strawberries*
Yum Yum Wreath*
Poppy Seed Bread* Sandwiches
Krispy Cheese Wafers*
Sugared Pecans*   Melting Moments*
Hot Cider Punch*   Coffee

AFTER-CHURCH BRUNCH

Friends will especially enjoy being together after a meaningful Christmas church service. The mood is set, the guests are already out and dressed, so you have only to extend the joy with a holiday brunch.

Hot and Spicy Tomato Warmer*
Fresh Fruit and Cheese Tray
Brunch Sausage Ring*   Buttered Broccoli
Bruncheon Curried Egg Casserole*
Hash Brown Potato Casserole*
Colonial Cheese Biscuits*
Christmas Cookies*   Lemon Bars*
Coffee and Russian Tea

SHOPPER'S PAUSE LUNCHEON

Invite a few favorite friends to escape the hustle and bustle and experience the warmth of sharing the spirit of Christmas. Light a fire, play Christmas music and brew Christmas Boil (see index) on the stove. For a special touch have a small gift at each guest's place at the table.

White Wine   Vegetable Juice
Chicken-Cranberry Layered Salad*
Broccoli with Hollandaise Sauce
Hot Peach Half with Chutney
Easy Tea Muffins*
Meringues* with Coffee Ice Cream and Heath Bar Topping*
Coffee

AFTERNOON WINE AND CHEESE PARTY

Invite a neighborhood group for a late afternoon wine and cheese party. Light food, simple to prepare and done ahead, combined with several favorite cheeses, compliment a chilled glass of wine and provide a warm welcome to your home.

Some Favorite Cheeses with Fresh Fruit   Crackers
Irresistible Shrimp Mold*   Baked Artichoke Dip*
Pickled Mushrooms*   Sugared Pecans*
Mock Daiquiri Slushy*   Wines

PICNIC BY THE FIRE

Relax by an open fire with good friends. Keep the "picnic" small enough to allow everyone to enjoy the fire. This is a perfect way to entertain after skiing, caroling or watching the marathon.

Cream Cheese Quintet*
Skiers' Chowder*
Cheese Puffs*   Bread Sticks
Rainbow Layered Vegetable Salad*
Mud Pie*
Hot Buttered Rum*   Coffee   Red Wine

HOLIDAY COCKTAIL BUFFET

The cocktail party is . . . an opportunity to see old friends, to make new friends, to visit and to eat . . . and all within 2 or 3 hours.

Filet of Beef*
Baked Smithfield Ham*
Assorted Party Breads
Mustard Sauce for Cocktail Roast* **Mayonnaise** **Horseradish Sauce**
Vegetables with Vegetable Dip*
Christmas Oyster Mold*
Creamed Mushrooms* **Green Wonders***
Spicy Cheese Mold*
Tea Time Tassies* **Toasted Pecans***
Coffee — Assorted Drinks
(Use "Bountiful Harvest Centerpiece"* as "fruit tray")

TEENAGERS' PROGRESSIVE DINNER

Teenagers have the most fun when they are "on the move." Three or four friends will enjoy entertaining together with a course at each home. Depending on the location of the houses, they might travel by foot, car, bus or haywagon.

House I
Favorite Dipping Vegetables* with Vegetable Dip*
Fresh Fruit
Peanuts **Popcorn** **Pretzels**
Juice and Soft Drinks

House II
Best Barbequed Beef*
Freezer Slaw*
Southern Baked Beans*
Hot Cider Punch*

House III
"Make Your Own" Sundae
Pound Cake Wafers*

DINNER AT EIGHT

Whether elegant or informal, no invitation is more complimentary or more enthusiastically received than "come for dinner." With everyone seated around the table, the pace is slower, conversation is more stimulating and guests are delighted with the opportunity to truly "visit" with each other. A favorite way to entertain!

Yummy Cream Cheese Hors d'Oeuvres*
Caviar Consomme*
All-Time Favorite Shrimp with Artichokes*
Asparagus Mold*
Broiled Tomato Halves **Wild Rice Casserole***
Serendipity Rolls*
World's Best Lemon Souffle*
Wine **Coffee**

"BRING THE FAMILY" PARTY

Children and grandparents welcome an invitation that includes them in a holiday party. One of the best ways to enrich and deepen friendships is to know the family of your friends. Plan an entertaining activity for the children, and remember to provide extra chairs for older guests. Everyone will enjoy gathering around the piano to sing carols. Your family party will become a favorite Christmas tradition.

Favorite Taco Dip*

Herb Chicken* Nuggets   Ham Biscuits

Waldorf Salad

Miniature Zucchini Souffle* Squares

Vegetable Strips — Stuffed Celery

Giant Chocolate Chip Cookies*

Holiday Eggnog* for Adults   Banana Crush Punch* for Children

Celophane-wrapped Gingerbread Boys and Girls* to take home

DROP BY FOR DESSERT

Dazzle your guests with a dessert extravaganza! Choose desserts with a colorful, interesting variety of flavors, textures and temperatures. Use your finest china, linen and silver and make it an elegant, unforgettable treat for dessert lovers.

Black Bottom Pie*

Pumpkin Roll*

Favorite Pound Cake*   Christmas Cookies*

Dessert Cheeses and Fruit

Coffee   Russian Tea

CHRISTMAS EVE WITH THE FAMILY

The air is charged with excitement—decorations, familiar and loved, are in place—the gifts are under the tree and out-of-town family has arrived. After weeks of anticipation, it is Christmas Eve. Serve an early supper; gather the family around the tree to sing carols, to read a favorite story or poem, and to end the evening by reading the Christmas story (Luke 2). Make this a special time with emphasis on the true meaning of Christmas. Consider sharing this evening by including a few friends who do not have families of their own.

Baked Artichoke Dip*

Seafood Gumbo*

Meal-in-One Sandwich*

Mixed Fruit (Grapefruit and Mandarin Oranges)

Tangy Winter Fruit Salad Dressing*

Banana Split Cake*

Coffee

SOUTHERN CHRISTMAS DINNER

Probably the most time-honored Christmas custom is the Christmas dinner. The aroma of good food in the kitchen, the yule log burning in the fireplace and those we cherish most, gathered together to share a meal . . . this is the Joy of Christmas.

Turkey* — Gravy* — Dressing*
Christmas Aspic-Cucumber Mold* or Cranberry Salad*
Sweet Potato Souffle* in Orange Shells
Tiny English Peas with Mushrooms or Broccoli with Hollandaise
Simply Rice*
Scalloped Oysters*
Assorted Relishes
Prize Fruitcake* or Favorite Pound Cake (Williamsburg)* or
Surprise Cake*
Old Fashioned Ambrosia*
Coffee — Tea — Champagne

NEW YEAR'S BOWL BUFFET

New Year's Day is a great time for a party for enthusiastic football fans who especially enjoy watching the bowl games with friends. Since guests usually choose to eat at different times, plan a menu that can be left on the table for several hours and eaten on trays in front of the television.

3 Kinds of Basic Quiches*
Crunchy Vegetable Marinate*
"Make Your Own" Ham Sandwich
Winter Curried Fruit*
Carrot Cake*   Super Duper Brownies*
Coffee   Wine   Assorted Beverages

THE TRADITIONAL NEW YEAR'S DAY "GOOD LUCK DINNER"

Baked Ham* with Raisin Sauce*
Tangy Tomato Aspic*
Hoppin' John*   Collards
Cornbread or Spoon Bread*
Maple Pecan Pie*

TWAS THE DAY AFTER CHRISTMAS

LEFTOVERS — TASTY AGAIN

Beef: Beef Sukiyaki*, vegetable soup, sandwiches or hash. **Note:** Reheat **rare** meat by lining a baking pan with green lettuce leaves. Top with layers of meat slices; then, top with another leaf blanket. Warm in slow oven.

Ham: Hearty Ham Chowder*, Ham Rolls*, Basic Quiche*, Ham and Crabmeat*, After Christmas Ham and Turkey Casserole*. Mince with pickles and mayonnaise for sandwich spread — add to omelets — make ham 'n eggs benedict — use the ham bone for soup.

Turkey and Chicken: Divine Chicken Divan*, Lemon-Turkey Bake*, Chicken-Cranberry Layered Salad*, Best Ever Chicken Salad*, Turkey Soup* or Baked Chicken Sandwich*. Add to quiches — make sandwiches — make Brunswick stew — serve turkey with gravy over cornbread or waffles.

Cheese: Soften with red wine, add cream cheese and make a cheese ball. Cover with crushed pecans and use for a party.

Eggs: Yolks: Vanilla Custard*, cream pies or mayonnaise. Whites: Meringues*, Cheese Puff* or Divine Divinity*. **Note:** Leftover egg whites and yolks can be frozen for up to 4 months. Freeze the whites as they are. Add ¼ teaspoon salt to every ¼ cup of yolks before freezing.

Vegetables: Vegetable soup or add to Basic Quiche*.

Mashed Potatoes: Make rolls, vichyssoise or Potato-Mushroom Casserole*. **Note:** To reheat a baked potato, dip in hot water and bake again in a moderate oven.

Cranberries: Make Cranberry-Apple Treat* or with cranberry sauce make Cranberry Salad*, Chicken-Cranberry Layered Salad* or Baked Bananas-Cranberry Casserole*. **Note:** Fresh cranberries can be frozen but should be used within a month.

Bread: Cheese Strata*, Cheese Puffs*, croutons, French toast, bread pudding. Freeze bread crumbs for later use in dressings or casserole toppings — cut out stale bread slices with cookie cutters and tie on an outside tree for the birds.

Pound Cake: Make Trifle*. Toast slices for breakfast — top with ice cream and chocolate sauce for dessert.

Beverages: Beer: Boil shrimp. Coffee: Make Irish Coffee* or mocha desserts. Wine: Use as a flavoring or to make a marinade.

CLEAN-UP

Candle Wax: To remove candle wax on fabric, first peel off any lumps of hard wax. Place a piece of blotter, absorbent towel or brown paper bag over and under the spot. Press with a hot iron. The paper will absorb the hot wax. Another method is to apply cube of ice for a few seconds; carefully scrape away wax with fingernail. (Repeat ice process as needed.)

Wine Stains: In 100% cotton, polyester and cotton blends, and permanent press fabrics, sponge stain with full-strength vinegar. Wash and dry as directed on manufacturer's care tag instructions. Treat as quickly as possible, since stain is difficult to remove after 24 hours. Another method is to pour salt on stain immediately. Later rub spot in cold water.

Ball Point Pen Ink: Before washing spray with hair spray.

China and Glass: To remove stubborn stains and give glassware a sparkle, clean with full-strength vinegar.

Lamp Shades: A piece of fresh bread will clean any lampshade except plastic ones. Just rub it over the shade — magic!

Alcohol Spots, Rings On Wood: Rub spot with cigarette ashes and then a cloth dipped in salad oil or cream wax. Always clean surfaces and polish.

Scratches On Wood: Rub in furniture wax with very, extra fine steel wool very gently. Polish or buff with soft cloth. Try covering a scratch by using a magic marker type pen in color of finish. (Test color underneath!)

Water Mark On Wood: Place thick blotter over the water mark and press with warm iron.

 # Recipes

APPETIZERS

BAKED ARTICHOKE DIP

8½-ounce can artichokes hearts,
chopped and drained

1 cup mayonnaise
1 cup Parmesan cheese, grated

Thoroughly mix all ingredients, and bake 20 minutes at 350°. Serve hot with crackers or toast rounds.

HEARTY CORNED BEEF DIP

1 pound round loaf pumpernickel
2 cups mayonnaise
3 teaspoons chives, chopped
3 tablespoons parsley flakes
3 teaspoons dry Italian seasoning

3 teaspoons dill weed
¾ pound can corned beef, broken up
½ cup sour cream

Hollow out loaf of bread and break bread core into bite-size pieces. Mix remaining ingredients to make dip. Fill hollowed-out space with corned beef mix and serve with bread bites.

HORSEY SHRIMP DIP

¾ cup shrimp, boiled, cleaned, and
chopped
3 tablespoons cream style
horseradish

4 tablespoons Hellman's
mayonnaise

Mix mayonnaise and horseradish. Add more or less of each, depending on how "hot or runny" you prefer. Add shrimp. Serve with Triscuits. Serves 6-8.

SPINACH DIP

1 package frozen chopped spinach,
cooked and drained
½ cup water
½ teaspoon salt
1 cup sour cream

1 cup mayonnaise
¼ teaspoon thyme
1 tablespoon onion, chopped
1 package Knorr's Vegetable Soup
Mix

Cook frozen spinach in water with salt; drain thoroughly in colander. Add sour cream, mayonnaise, thyme, onion and soup mix. Mix thoroughly. Chill and serve with crackers. May add ½ small can water chestnuts, sliced very thin.

FAVORITE TACO DIP

2 8-ounce cans Frito Lay bean dip
3 medium ripened avocados
Lemon juice
Salt and pepper
1 8-ounce carton sour cream
½ cup Hellman's mayonnaise

1 1¼-ounce package taco mix
1 cup green onion tops, chopped
1 cup fresh tomatoes, chopped
1 7¼-ounce can ripe olives, sliced
1 8-ounce package sharp cheese, grated

Mash bean dip and spread to edges of a glass sandwich tray with lip. Peel and mash avocado, season with a splash of lemon juice, salt and pepper. Mix well and spread on top of bean dip layer. Mix sour cream, mayonnaise, and taco mix, and spread on top of avocado layer. Sprinkle on layer of onions, tomatoes and olives. Top with grated cheese, and chill for several hours. Serve with traditional Tostados.

DOWN EAST CLAM DIP

1 8-ounce package cream cheese
3 tablespoons mayonnaise
5 tablespoons sour cream
¼ teaspoon lemon juice

Dash of Worcestershire
2 tablespoons onion, grated
1 6½-ounce can clams, minced

Allow cream cheese to soften at room temperature. Mash and mix next 5 ingredients until smooth and dip consistency, using some of the clam juice to help soften cream cheese. Season to taste. Add drained clams.

Favorite Variation: Mix 1 8-ounce cream cheese and 1 can drained minced clams. Use liquid from clams to soften cream cheese to desired consistency. Season with Worcestershire and Tabasco to taste.

VEGETABLE DIP

1 cup mayonnaise
2 teaspoons tarragon vinegar
½ teaspoon salt
⅓ teaspoon curry powder
⅛ teaspoon thyme flakes

2 tablespoons chili sauce
1 teaspoon grated onion
1 teaspoon onion, finely chopped
Dash of pepper

Mix thoroughly and refrigerate. Serve with carrot and celery sticks, cauliflower and broccoli flowerets, squash and cucumber slices, and any other fresh vegetables that may be in season.

FAVORITE DIPPING VEGETABLES

Asparagus	Mushrooms	Cherry tomatoes
Artichokes	Carrots	Eggplant spears
Green beans	Cucumbers	Snow peas
Broccoli	Cauliflower	Yellow squash
Celery	Radishes	Zucchini

EYE OF THE ROUND COCKTAIL ROAST

1 5-pound roast
Tenderizer
1 cup Italian dressing

½ teaspoon Lawry's Seasoning Salt
1 tablespoon olive oil

Put a generous sprinkling of tenderizer on one side of the roast for half hour, then on the other for half hour. Marinate roast in the remaining ingredients in refrigerator overnight. Turn once before going to bed. Cook either in foil, wrapped tightly, or in roaster, covered, at 200° for 4 or 5 hours. Allow to cool before slicing or take back to the butcher to be sliced, if very thin slices are preferred.

Favorite Variations in Cooking: 1. Wrap in foil with a little sauce. Bake at 350° for 2 hours until meat thermometer reaches 140° for rare or desired doneness. 2. Preheat oven to 500°. Wipe roast. Salt and pepper. Cook roast five minutes per pound; then, cut off oven and leave in the oven until cool. Do not open door of oven until cool. Take out in 2 hours.

MUSTARD SAUCE FOR COCKTAIL ROAST

1 tablespoon butter, melted
1 egg
¼ cup brown sugar

3 tablespoons sugar
2 tablespoons dry mustard
⅓ cup vinegar

Melt butter. Cool. Beat egg, sugars and mustard well with mixer. Beat in vinegar and butter. Cook over **low** heat 3 or 4 minutes until thickened, stirring constantly. Cool and refrigerate. Serve cold or hot with meats.

PUNGENT CHICKEN WINGS

1½ pounds broiler-fryer wings (8-
    10)
2 teaspoons cornstarch
1½ teaspoons 4-spice powder**
2 tablespoons sugar
1 tablespoon peanut oil

2 tablespoons dry, medium or sweet
    sherry
¼ teaspoon pepper flakes
1 tablespoon minced fresh ginger
    root
½ cup soy sauce
½ cup water

**4 spice powder: ¼ teaspoons each cinnamon, ginger, cloves, and nutmeg

Wash wings, drain and dry; cut into two parts at joints. (Do not use tips.) In a medium saucepan stir together the cornstarch, spice powder, sugar, oil and sherry until blended; stir in all ingredients but wings. Bring to a boil stirring constantly. Add wings and boil; cover and simmer 20 minutes. Leave in sauce and reheat just before serving.

Favorite Variation: Add garlic powder if desired. Wings are also delicious marinated in only Kikkoman Soy Sauce; then, bake at 325° for 30 minutes (baste often with marinade).

HAM ROLLS

2 sticks butter, softened
1-2 tablespoons horseradish mustard
2 tablespoons poppy seeds
1 teaspoon Worcestershire
1 medium onion, minced

3 dozen Pepperidge Farm finger
  rolls
16-ounces cooked ham, thinly sliced
2 cups Swiss cheese, grated

Mix butter, mustard, poppy seeds, Worcestershire and onion. Split package of rolls horizontally through the center. Spread butter mixture on both sides of rolls. Layer bottom half with ham. Sprinkle Swiss cheese on top of ham. Replace tops. Bake at 400° for 10-15 minutes. These freeze well. Cut into individual rolls before freezing so a few may be used at a time.

SOUTHERN SAUSAGE BISCUITS

2 cups Bisquick
½ cup water
1 pound sausage (hot), cooked and
  drained thoroughly

1 cup New York State sharp
  Cheddar cheese, grated

Mix well, roll into tiny balls (about the size of a nickel). Cook at 400° for 10-15 minutes. Drain on a wire rack covered with a paper towel. They may be frozen. To reheat, bake for 10 minutes at 325°.

KRISPY CHEESE WAFERS

½ pound sharp cheese, grated
1 stick butter, softened
1 cup flour

½ teaspoon salt
¼ teaspoon cayenne pepper
2 cups Rice Krispies

Mix together and make into very small balls. Place on cookie sheet; flatten balls with hand to make wafer size. Cook 7-9 minutes or more at 400° until they are slightly brown. Remove from cookie sheet immediately.

Favorite Variation: Add ½ cup walnuts; ½ teaspoon garlic salt; 6 slices bacon, fried and crumbled; 2 tablespoons cooking oil, and 4-5 teaspoons cold water. Bake at 375° for 10-12 minutes.

RIPE OLIVE COCKTAIL SANDWICHES

3 3-ounce packages cream cheese
1 can chopped ripe olives (small)
1 small onion, grated
1 cup nut meats, broken
Salt and pepper to taste

Dash of lemon juice
Dash of red pepper
½ cup Miracle Whip Salad
  Dressing

Mix first 7 ingredients; then mix with the salad dressing. Makes about 24 party sandwiches.

SALMON SOUFFLE

4 slices bread, cubed
½ cup milk
3 tablespoons butter, melted
1 16-ounce can salmon, drained
  (remove bone and skin)
3 tablespoons lemon juice

2 teaspoons onion, minced
1 teaspoon salt
¼ teaspoon pepper
½ teaspoon paprika
4 eggs, separated and beaten
¼ teaspoon cream of tartar

Mix everything but beaten egg whites and cream of tartar. Stir well to moisten bread. Fold in egg whites (stiffly beaten with ¼ teaspoon cream of tartar). Bake in 1½ quart dish at 350° for 45 minutes. May be served as an appetizer with crackers, a fish course or a luncheon entree.

CHRISTMAS OYSTER ROLL

2 8-ounce packages cream cheese	½ small onion, grated
2 teaspoons Worcestershire	3 tablespoons mayonnaise
⅛ teaspoon garlic powder	⅛ teaspoon salt
2 cans smoked oysters, drained and finely chopped	¼ cup fresh parsley, chopped

Cream together cream cheese, Worcestershire, garlic powder, onion, mayonnaise, and salt. Spread mixture on waxed paper until it is about 12x8 inches and less than ½ inch thick. Chill in refrigerator about an hour. Spread oysters on top of cheese mixture, and roll up into a log. Roll log in chopped parsley and chill in refrigerator for 24 hours before serving. Serve with crackers. Serves 10-25, depending on what else you serve.

MARINATED SHRIMP

1½ large Bermuda onions, thinly sliced	1 teaspoon prepared mustard
2 pounds shrimp, boiled and cleaned	1 teaspoon salt
2 cups vinegar	½ teaspoon pepper
1 cup cooking oil	2 cloves garlic, crushed
¼ cup Worcestershire	1 teaspoon paprika
	2 small onions, diced

Boil shrimp, drain, peel and devein. Slice Bermuda onions and separate into rings. Alternate shrimp and onions in container. Combine remaining ingredients and mix well. Pour over shrimp and onions and marinate overnight. Drain to serve. Serves 8 as a salad served on lettuce or about 14-20 as an appetizer.

IRRESISTIBLE SHRIMP MOLD

3 cups shrimp, boiled and cleaned	Salt and pepper to taste
¾ cup Miracle Whip Salad Dressing	3 or 4 hard boiled eggs, grated
¼ cup mayonnaise	1 tablespoon onion, grated
1 package unflavored gelatin	1 tablespoon lemon juice
¼ cup cold water	½ teaspoon Worcestershire
1 cup celery, finely chopped	Dash of red pepper
	Dash of Accent

Boil, peel and devein shrimp; finely chop. Have Miracle Whip and mayonnaise at room temperature; then, heat in double boiler over hot water. Dissolve gelatin in cold water and add to hot mayonnaise and Miracle Whip. Mix all ingredients and pour into a slightly greased mold*. Make at least one day ahead. Garnish with parsley to serve with crackers or melba toast. *Use glass or plastic mold, not metal. Mayonnaise-seafood dishes turn gray-green in metal containers.

SPICY CHEESE MOLD

1 8-ounce package cream cheese
1 jar very sharp cheese (Old
   English)
⅓ to ½ pound Roquefort cheese

¼ teaspoon red pepper
3 teaspoons Worcestershire
¾ teaspoon garlic salt (more if
   preferred)
¾ cup pecans, chopped

Let cheeses stand at room temperature about 2 hours. Mix in mix master at slow speed, until cheeses are blended. Add seasoning while mixing. Stir in one half pecans. Put in refrigerator until thoroughly cooled and firm. Wet hands with cold water and make into ball. Roll in remaining pecans; pat on, if necessary. Refrigerate until serving time.

Favorite Variation: Crab Cheese Loaf: Eliminate pecans, and use only ¼ pound of Roquefort cheese. Add 1 additional 8-ounce package cream cheese, 1 tablespoon mayonnaise, 1 tablespoon lemon juice and 1 8-ounce can of crabmeat. Mix well and put in loaf pan, greased with salad oil. (Cross wax paper on bottom.) Chill until firm, remove from loaf pan and invert. Decorate top by alternating strips of chopped parsley, grated egg yolks and paprika.

YUMMY CREAM CHEESE HORS D'OEUVRES

1 18-ounce jar pineapple preserves
1 18-ounce jar apple jelly
1 4-ounce jar horseradish
1 1-ounce can dry mustard

1 tablespoon cracked black pepper
   (or less)
1 8-ounce package cream cheese

Mix first 5 ingredients and chill in refrigerator. Pour over cream cheese. Serve with Triscuits or bland crackers.

TOASTED PECANS

3 cups pecan halves   ½ stick butter

Place pecans on baking sheet and dot with butter. Bake at 275° for 1 hour.
Favorite Variation: Add 1-2 teaspoons salt.

PICKLED MUSHROOMS

¾ cup water
¾ cup vinegar
½ teaspoon leaf marjoram
¼ teaspoon whole cloves
½ teaspoon celery seed
½ teaspoon mustard seed

1 teaspoon salt
Few drops hot sauce
1 tablespoon sugar (rounded)
3 medium onions
½ to 1 pound fresh mushrooms
¼ cup olive oil

Mix the first 9 ingredients together to make a sauce. Slice onions and cook in sauce for 5 minutes. Add mushrooms and cook 5 minutes longer. Remove mushrooms. Add olive oil to liquid and onions. Bring to boil and pour over mushrooms. Refrigerate 3 hours.

Favorite Variation: Use drained, canned whole mushrooms, but do not boil, just marinate.

CREAMED MUSHROOMS

1 pound fresh mushrooms	½ teaspoon lemon juice
1½ tablespoons butter	2 tablespoons flour
2 tablespoons chicken stock	¼ cup consommé
1 small onion, minced	½ cup cream
¾ teaspoons parsley, chopped	1 tablespoon sherry

Slice mushrooms. Melt butter and stock. Simmer onions and parsley until soft. Add mushrooms and lemon juice and simmer 10 minutes. Dust with flour; add consommé and cream and stir until thickens. Simmer 15 minutes and add sherry. Salt and pepper to taste. Serve in chafing dish with toast cups or pastry cups.

GREEN WONDERS

2 10-ounce packages chopped spinach, cooked and drained	¾ cup butter, melted
	½ cup grated Parmesan cheese
2 cups herbed stuffing mix	1 tablespoon garlic salt
2 large onions, finely chopped	1½ teaspoons thyme flakes
5 eggs, beaten	Pepper to taste

Mix all ingredients together in bowl. Chill 2 hours. Shape into small balls, place on cookie sheet and freeze. When frozen, pack in freezer containers to use as needed. Bake 20 to 30 minutes at 350°. Makes about 70. Serves about 20.

EMERGENCY APPETIZERS

Tomato-Oysters: Cut a cherry tomato into quarters, but do not cut deeply enough to separate sections. Stuff center with a smoked oyster.

Cream Cheese Quintet: Arrange 5 packages (3-ounce size) cream cheese on a narrow tray. Coat 1 block with toasted sesame seed; drizzle soy sauce over top. Press chopped chives into second cheese block to cover all the surfaces generously. Spoon canned taco sauce or chili sauce over third cheese block. Top fourth with Worcestershire sauce and sprinkle with Parmesan cheese. Top fifth with salmon caviar. Serve with crisp crackers.

Speared Fruit: Spear a chunk of pineapple, a strawberry, a melon ball, and several green seedless grapes on a long wooden pick. Serve picks in a bowl on crushed ice. (Also excellent garnishes when sprinkled with brown sugar and curry. Heat slightly in 450° oven.)

Lemon Apples: Cut unpeeled apples into wedges. Slice away core. "Marinate" in thawed frozen lemonade concentrate for several hours.

Edam Balls: Slice off the top of an Edam cheese. Scoop out balls of cheese with a melon ball cutter. Refill the Edam shell with the cheese balls. Place toothpicks nearby.

Dipping Vegetables: Select fresh, crunchy vegetables; wash thoroughly; cut in rounds, spears, or leave whole; keep crisp on ice until serving time; drain thoroughly; and arrange on tray. Serve with your favorite sauce.

Sugared Strawberries: Wash whole uncapped strawberries. Serve with a bowl of confectioners sugar for dipping. Another quick dip is either sour cream or whipped cream flavored with confectioners sugar and frozen orange juice concentrate.

SOUPS AND SANDWICHES

GAZPACHO

½ cup celery, diced
½ cup green pepper, diced
½ cup onion, diced
1 cup thinly sliced tomatoes
½ cup thinly sliced cucumbers
1 10½-ounce can tomato soup,
   undiluted
1 soup can water
1½ cups vegetable juice
   (V-8)

1 tablespoon wine vinegar
1 tablespoon Italian dressing
   (commercial)
Garlic salt to taste
¼ teaspoon salt
⅛ teaspoon pepper
4 dashes hot sauce
1 dash Worcestershire

Combine all ingredients in a bowl. Cover, refrigerate at least 4 hours. Stir gently. Serve in chilled bowls or mugs. Top with a dollop of sour cream. Serves 6-8.

Favorite Variation: QUICK AND EASY — To 2 cups V-8 juice, add the above vegetables. Chill and, just before serving, add 1 tablespoon lemon juice.

SKIER'S CHOWDER

1 pound roll of hot pork sausage
2 1-pound cans kidney beans
1 1-pound, 13-ounce can tomatoes,
   broken up
1 quart water
1 large onion, chopped
1 bay leaf

1½ teaspoons seasoning salt
½ teaspoon garlic salt
½ teaspoon thyme
⅛ teaspoon pepper
1 cup potatoes, diced
½ green pepper, chopped

Cook sausage until brown and drain thoroughly. In a large pot combine beans, tomatoes, water, onion, bay leaf, seasoned salt, garlic salt, thyme and pepper. Add sausage and simmer, covered, for 1-1½ hours. Add potatoes and green pepper. Cook covered, 15-20 minutes, until potatoes are tender. Remove bay leaf. Makes 8 servings.

SEAFOOD GUMBO

5 tablespoons bacon drippings
6 tablespoons flour
2 onions, chopped
1½ cups celery, finely chopped
1 pod garlic, pressed
1 large can tomatoes (20-ounces) or
   2 fresh large tomatoes, crushed
1 15-ounce can tomato sauce
5 or 6 cups water
3 teaspoons salt

1 teaspoon pepper
1 10-ounce package cut okra
2 pounds shrimp, boiled, peeled and
   deveined
1 pint oysters (or 1 quart,
   depending on how much you
   like oysters)
3 tablespoons Worcestershire
1 cup rice, cooked

Make a roux of bacon drippings and flour. Bubble and cook slowly. Add onions, celery and garlic and cook 5 minutes with roux. Add tomatoes, tomato sauce, water, salt and pepper. Cook for one hour, stirring occasionally to keep from sticking. Add okra, and cook 20 minutes longer. Add shrimp and cook 5 minutes. Add oysters and Worcestershire and allow to heat thoroughly. Serve over a little rice in each bowl. Serves 8-10.

Favorite Variation: For a shrimp gumbo, substitute additional tomatoes for ½ of the water. Vary the flavor by adding one or more of the following seasonings: thyme, bay leaf, chopped parsley. Eliminate oysters.

HOT AND SPICY TOMATO WARMER

1 cup V-8 juice   1 beef bouillon cube

Heat until bouillon cube melts. Serve in mug.

ELEGANCE FROM A CAN*

After-Work Clam Chowder: Combine 1 can Potato Soup, 1 can milk, 2 shredded carrots, 1 (6½-ounce) can minced clams with juice and ½ teaspoon thyme. Heat to boiling, but do not scald. Add 1 tablespoon butter and serve with 2 strips cooked, crumbled bacon on top. Serves 2-3.

Crab Bisque Supreme: Mix 1 can Cream of Mushroom Soup, 1 can Cream of Asparagus Soup, 1½ cans milk, 1 cup light cream. Heat just to boiling. Add 1 cup crab meat, drained and flaked (or 1 7½-ounce can of crab meat) and heat thoroughly. Remove from heat, stir in ¼ cup sherry, 2 tablespoons butter and dash of hot pepper sauce. Serve sprinkled with paprika and chopped parsley. Makes 6-8 servings.

Hearty Ham Chowder: Mix 1 can Cream of Mushroom Soup, 1 can Cream of Asparagus Soup, 1 can Cream of Pea Soup plus 1 cup leftover ham, chopped. Add 3 cans of milk. Heat until hot, stirring constantly. Serves 6-8.

Cream of Spinach Soup: Combine 1 can Cheddar Cheese Soup, 1 can water, 1 tablespoon beef bouillon powder and several dashes nutmeg. Add ½ pound fresh chopped mushrooms and ½ package frozen chopped spinach. Simmer all ingredients until mushrooms are tender. Top with Parmesan cheese. Serves 4.

Turkey Soup: Mix 1 can Cream of Mushroom Soup mixed with 1 can Cream of Chicken Soup, 2 cans milk or cream and ¾ cup diced leftover turkey. Top with fresh chopped parsley. Serves 4.

Caviar Consommé: Jell 2 cans consommé for several hours in refrigerator. Fill small bowls or cups with consommé, and top **each** with a tablespoon of sour cream and a teaspoon of salmon caviar. Serves 4-6.

*Note: Directions for 10-ounce to 10-¾-ounce cans: One "can" milk, cream or water indicates one **soup** can.

BAKED CHICKEN SANDWICHES

16 slices of bread, crusts trimmed
1 stick butter, softened
½ pound fresh mushrooms, sliced
   (canned may be used)
2 cups chicken (white meat),
   cooked and diced
3 hard boiled eggs, chopped
⅓ cup ripe olives, sliced

¾ cup mayonnaise
2 tablespoons onion, chopped
1 10½-ounce can cream of chicken
   soup, undiluted
1 cup sour cream
2 tablespoons sherry
Paprika to sprinkle on top

Sauté mushrooms in 2 tablespoons butter. Butter both sides of bread with remaining butter and place 8 slices in 9 x 13 inch pan. Cover bread with mixture of mushrooms, chicken, eggs, olives, mayonnaise and onion. Arrange 8 other slices of bread on top. Combine soup, sour cream and sherry. Pour on top. Bake at 325° for 30 minutes. Serves 8.

OPEN-FACE JUMBO

8 strips of bacon
2 3-ounce packages cream cheese
½ stick butter, softened
2 teaspoons lemon juice
1 tablespoon onion, grated
1 teaspoon dried parsley

1 teaspoon Worcestershire
1 cup cooked turkey, diced
4 English muffins
8 large slices tomato
8 slices Cheddar cheese or 1 cup,
   grated

Cook bacon and reserve. Cream together cream cheese, butter, juice, onion, parsley, and Worcestershire. Add turkey bits and mix well. Put mixture on muffin halves. Top with tomato slices, salt and pepper to taste. Top with cheese. Broil on bottom rack of oven for 15 minutes at 350°. Top with bacon slices. Serves 4 generously.

LAZY DAISY SANDWICH MEAL

8 deviled egg sandwiches
Lettuce
16 slices tomato
1 pound crab meat
1 cup mayonnaise

2 tablespoons chili sauce
1 tablespoon onion, finely chopped
1 tablespoon green pepper, chopped
1 hard boiled egg, chopped

Make 8 deviled egg sandwiches and cut off crust. Place each on a lettuce leaf and top with 2 slices tomato. On each, put a scoop of fresh crab meat. Be sure to check crab meat for bits of shell. Top entire sandwich with dressing made from mayonnaise, chili sauce, onion, green pepper and egg. If you are in a hurry, substitute bottled Thousand Island Salad Dressing to which you have added the chopped, boiled egg. Serves 8.

MEAL-IN-ONE-SANDWICH

½ cup green pepper, chopped
½ cup onion, chopped
1 cup mayonnaise
1 cup sharp cheese, grated

Pepper to taste
1 teaspoon salt
Fresh tomatoes and squash
8 slices of bread, toasted

Make sauce by mixing green pepper, onion, mayonnaise, cheese, salt and pepper. Slice fresh tomatoes and tender raw yellow squash (or zucchini) on toast. Put sauce on top and broil until sauce is melted. Sauce keeps well in a sealed container in refrigerator for a week. Complete Sunday night supper with a fruit salad.

Favorite Variation: Sauce may be spread on toasted hamburger bun and broiled but use only ⅓ cup mayonnaise. Top each with 2 crisply fried strips of bacon.

SALADS

CHRISTMAS ASPIC — CUCUMBER MOLD

1 envelope gelatin	¾ cup boiling water
1¾ cups V-8 juice	¼ cup mayonnaise
½ cup onion, finely minced	2 teaspoons cider vinegar
¼ cup green olives, chopped	½ teaspoon salt
½ teaspoon salt	1 8-ounce carton sour cream
1 tablespoon lemon juice	2 medium cucumbers, seeded and
Dash Worcestershire	chopped very small
1 3-ounce package lime Jello	

Soften gelatin in a little V-8 juice; dissolve in remainder of heated juice. Add onion, olives, salt, lemon juice and Worcestershire; mix thoroughly. Pour into a mold and refrigerate until set. Meanwhile, dissolve Jello in boiling water. Remove from stove and mix thoroughly with mayonnaise, vinegar, salt, sour cream and cucumber. When first layer has congealed, pour this on top for a second layer. Refrigerate until congealed. Serves 12. Colorful red and green salad!

TANGY TOMATO ASPIC

1 16-ounce can tomatoes, mashed	1½ envelopes gelatin
½ cup sugar	½ cup cold water
½ cup vinegar	½ cup green pepper, chopped
1 small onion, chopped	½ cup pecans, chopped
Salt and pepper to taste	¼ cup celery, chopped
	1 tablespoon India relish

Simmer tomatoes, sugar, vinegar, onion, salt and pepper for ½ hour. Add 1½ packages of gelatin dissolved in ½ cup cold water. When cool, add green pepper, nuts, celery and relish. Congeal in 8 to 10 individual molds.

ASPARAGUS AND ARTICHOKES

1 can asparagus spears, drained	¼ cup water
1 8½-ounce can artichoke hearts	½ teaspoon salt
(cut in half)	6 cloves
⅓ cup wine vinegar	2 cinnamon sticks
¼ cup sugar	¼ teaspoon celery seeds

Mix vinegar, sugar, water, and seasonings; heat until sugar dissolves. Marinate asparagus for 24 hours, adding artichokes for last 12 hours. Drain and serve as cold vegetable or salad. Serves 4.

ASPARAGUS MOLD

2 envelopes unflavored gelatin
½ cup cold water
1 can asparagus soup, undiluted
½ cup Green Goddess salad
    dressing
3 3-ounce packages cream cheese,
    softened

1 tablespoon onion, finely grated
1 cup stuffed green olives, sliced
1½ cups celery, finely diced
2 10½-ounce cans asparagus tips,
    drained
½ cup pecans, broken

Soften gelatin in water. Heat soup to boiling point and stir into gelatin. Stir until gelatin is dissolved. Mix together cream cheese and salad dressing and add to soup mixture. Stir in onion, olives, celery, asparagus tips and pecans. Spoon into an oiled 6-cup mold. Chill until set. **Party Note:** Mold in fish mold, add olives for eyes and halves of thinly sliced cucumbers for scales. A Christmas "wreath" mold with a pimento "bow" is delicious **and** decorative for a Christmas luncheon. Serves 12.

COOL CARROTS

2 bunches carrots, peeled and
    thinly sliced or baby carrots
½ teaspoon salt
1 10½-ounce can tomato soup,
    undiluted
¾ cup vinegar
¾ cup sugar

½ cup vegetable oil
1 teaspoon dry mustard
1 bell pepper (green or red),
    chopped
1 jar sour pickled onions, cocktail
    small size (pearl)
1 teaspoon herb seasonings
    (optional)

Boil carrots 10 minutes in water with ½ teaspoon salt. Drain. Boil the next 6 ingredients for 5 minutes. Remove from stove and add drained sour pickled onions and herb seasonings. Pour over carrots. Marinate 6-8 hours. Serve hot or cold.

Favorite Variation: Use canned baby carrots, drained.

FREEZER SLAW

1 large head cabbage, shredded or
    chopped
1 large onion, chopped
⅞ cup sugar
1 cup white vinegar

¾ cup salad oil
1 tablespoon salt or less
2 teaspoons sugar
1 teaspoon dry mustard
1 teaspoon celery seeds

Place ½ of the shredded cabbage in a bowl. Add chopped onion. Place rest of cabbage on top of onion and sprinkle with ⅞ cup of sugar. Heat vinegar, salad oil, salt, 2 teaspoons sugar, dry mustard and celery seeds to boiling. Pour over cabbage and cover at once. Refrigerate at least 4 hours. This slaw improves with age and keeps well in the refrigerator for 2 week . . . **freezes well, also.**

Note: For Christmas color, add a little pimento to slaw just before serving.

MARINATED CUCUMBERS AND ONIONS

6 cucumbers
4 onions
1 tablespoon salt

1 cup sugar
1 cup vinegar
1 8-ounce carton sour cream

Slice cucumbers and onions. Sprinkle with salt and let stand 6 hours. Drain. Mix sugar and vinegar. Dissolve; then, add sour cream. Mix, and pour over vegetables. Let stand 24 hours.

RAINBOW LAYERED VEGETABLE SALAD

½ head lettuce
Fresh spinach
4 hard-boiled eggs, sliced
Bacon bits
Fresh mushrooms, sliced
Squash, sliced
Cucumbers, sliced
Carrots, grated
Celery, chopped

Onions, chopped
1 10-ounce package frozen green
   peas
2 small packages Ranch dressing
   mix
2 8-ounce cartons sour cream
½ cup Hellman's mayonnaise
Bacon Bits
Cheese, grated (Swiss or Cheddar)
Croutons

Using a large, clear glass salad bowl, break lettuce in bottom. Add a layer of each: spinach, hard-boiled eggs, bacon bits, sliced mushrooms, sliced squash, sliced cucumbers, grated carrots, chopped celery, chopped onions, frozen green peas (that have been cooked 3-4 minutes and cooled). Spread dressing (Ranch dressing mix, sour cream and mayonnaise mixed together) over entire surface of vegetables and refrigerate for 4 to 6 hours.* Garnish with bacon bits, cheese and croutons.

Favorite Variation: Add a layer of green olives with pimento, water chestnuts, broccoli, etc. It is a complete meal when adding cooked and diced chicken or ham. (In a hurry — top with 1 pint Miracle Whip Salad Dressing straight from the jar.)

*Note: This salad keeps well and is best made a day or 8 hours ahead. It is as pretty as it is good if the layers are arranged artistically in contrasting colors that show through the glass bowl.

CRUNCHY VEGETABLE MARINATE

1½ cups vegetable oil
1 tablespoon sugar
1 cup cider vinegar
1 tablespoon dill weed
1 tablespoon Accent
1 teaspoon salt

1 teaspoon pepper
1 teaspoon garlic salt
Broccoli and cauliflower
   flowerettes
Tender sugar peas
Fresh mushrooms

Mix first 8 ingredients. Toss with a mixture of the above fresh vegetables (about a total of 6-8 cups). Refrigerate 24 hours, basting several times. Excellent salad or appetizer.

CRANBERRY SALAD

1½ envelopes gelatin	½ cup boiling water
¼ cup cold water	¼ teaspoon salt
¼ cup orange juice	⅓ cup celery, chopped
1 16-ounce can cranberry sauce	⅓ cup nuts, chopped
(whole berry)	⅓ cup unpeeled apple, chopped

Put gelatin in cold water and orange juice. Heat cranberry sauce in sauce pan to boiling point. Add hot water to gelatin, dissolve and add to hot cranberries. Let cool. Add salt, celery, nuts and apples. Pour into 1 quart mold.

Favorite Variations: Eliminate celery and apples and add drained mandarin oranges and/or crushed pineapple. Also good, for a sweeter salad, add 1 cup miniature marshmallows. Topping: "Frost" with same topping as Frosted Fruit Salad. Sprinkle top with additional pecans.

FROSTED FRUIT SALAD

1 package lemon Jello	2 cups bite-size marshmallows
1 package orange Jello	2 tablespoons flour
2 cups hot water	½ cup sugar
1½ cups cold water	1 egg, slightly beaten
Juice of lemon	2 tablespoons butter
1 20-ounce can crushed pineapple,	1 cup whipping cream, whipped
drained (save juice)	½ cup sharp cheese, grated
2 bananas, diced	

Dissolve Jellos in hot water; add cold water and lemon juice. Chill until partly thickened. Fold in pineapple, bananas, and marshmallows. Pour into 9 x 12 inch refrigerator dish. Chill until firm. Make topping for salad. Mix flour and sugar in heavy pan, then add egg and pineapple juice. Cook until thick. Add butter and cool. When cold, fold in whipped cream. Spread on salad and sprinkle with cheese. Serves 12-16.

PUDDING FROZEN FRUIT SALAD

1 3⅛-ounce package vanilla instant	1 16-ounce can fruit cocktail
pudding	½ pint whipping cream, whipped
1 20-ounce can crushed pineapple	¼-½ cup pecans, broken

Drain juices of pineapple and fruit cocktail. Use for liquid to make pudding. Make pudding according to package directions. Whip cream. Add fruit to pudding, and fold in cream. Add broken pecans pieces last. Freeze several hours. Makes 10 individual molds. For children, mold in small paper cups.

Favorite Variation: Add one diced banana.

Favorite Tips: Gelatin dishes should be eaten within 3 days; after this, they become rubbery.

TANGY WINTER FRUIT SALAD

1¼ cups sugar
⅔ cup vinegar
1-2 teaspoons dry mustard
1 tablespoon onion, grated

2 cups salad oil
2 tablespoons poppy or celery seed
2 teaspoons salt
Mixed fruit

Mix first four ingredients. Add oil slowly, stirring constantly, before adding seeds and salt. (Keep dressing in refrigerator until ready to serve.) Serve over any combination of the following: pineapple chunks, mandarin oranges, grapefruit sections, avocado, celery, grated coconut, raisins, bananas, sliced water chestnuts or pecans.

CHICKEN-CRANBERRY LAYERED SALAD

2 tablespoons gelatin
1 cup water
1 pound can cranberry sauce
    (whole berry)
¾ cup crushed pineapple, drained
½ cup pecans, broken
4 tablespoons lemon juice
1 cup mayonnaise

¾ teaspoon salt
2 cups diced cooked chicken or
    turkey
½ cup celery, diced
2 tablespoons fresh parsley,
    chopped
Pecans, chopped

Layer 1: Soften 1 tablespoon unflavored gelatin in ¼ cup cold water. Dissolve over hot water. Add one 1-pound can (2 cups) cranberry sauce, ¾ cup crushed pineapple (drain juice off), ½ cup broken pecans and 1 tablespoon lemon juice. Pour into an 8 x 8 inch Pyrex dish. Chill until firm.
Layer 2: Meanwhile, soften 1 tablespoon unflavored gelatin in ¼ cup cold water. Dissolve over hot water. Blend in 1 cup mayonnaise, ½ cup water, 3 tablespoons lemon juice and ¾ teaspoon salt. Add 2 cups diced cooked chicken or turkey, ½ cup diced celery and 2 tablespoons chopped parsley. Pour over first layer and chill until firm. Take out by cutting squares (red side up). Top with mayonnaise and pecans. Serves 12.

BEST EVER CHICKEN SALAD

5 cups cooked chicken, chopped
2 tablespoons salad oil
2 tablespoons orange juice
2 tablespoons vinegar
1 teaspoon salt
3 cups regular rice, cooked
1½ cups small seedless grapes

1½ cups celery, sliced
1 15¼-ounce can pineapple chunks,
    drained
1 11-ounce can mandarin orange
    sections, drained
1 cup slivered almonds, toasted
½ cup mayonnaise

Combine first 5 ingredients in a large bowl; let stand about 30 minutes to allow flavors to blend. Add remaining ingredients and toss gently. Yield: 10 to 12 servings.

Favorite Variation: Drain marinated chicken well, eliminate rice and add ½ cup whipping cream, whipped. Without the rice, it will serve only 6-8.

CHEESE AND EGGS

BRUNCHEON CURRIED EGG CASSEROLE

8 hard-boiled eggs
⅓ cup mayonnaise
¼ teaspoon dry mustard
½ teaspoon salt
½ teaspoon curry powder
½ teaspoon paprika
2 tablespoons butter
2 tablespoons flour

1½ cups milk
1 can frozen Shrimp Soup or 1
   10½-ounce can condensed
   shrimp soup, undiluted
½ cup sharp Cheddar cheese,
   grated
1 cup toasted bread crumbs
2 tablespoons butter, melted

Devil hard-boiled eggs with mixture of egg yolks, mayonnaise, mustard, salt, curry powder and paprika. Place in large shallow baking dish. Make sauce by melting 2 tablespoons butter; add flour and mix well. Add milk, shrimp soup and grated cheese. Stir well until smooth and cook slowly until thick. Pour this sauce over the eggs. Top with bread crumbs that have been tossed with 2 tablespoons melted butter. Bake at 350° for 25-30 minutes. Serves about 6.

Favorite Variation: Add 1 pound small, cooked shrimp for a more elegant dish.

CHEESE STRATA

8-10 slices bread
Butter
½ pound sharp Cheddar cheese,
   grated
2 cups milk

1 teaspoon salt
1 teaspoon Worcestershire
4 eggs, slightly beaten
1 teaspoon prepared mustard

Remove crust from bread and spread with butter. Put a layer of bread in casserole dish. Sprinkle with grated cheese. Add another layer of bread, sprinkle with cheese. Beat milk, salt, Worcestershire, eggs and mustard together. Pour over bread. Let stand several hours or overnight. Bake at 300° for 45 minutes or until set. Serves 8-10.

Favorite Variations: Between layers of bread, add 1 pound sausage that has been cooked, drained and crumbled or any of the following cooked items: chipped beef, ham, chicken, broccoli, spinach, zucchini or mushrooms. Good use of leftovers. Total amount of filling added should equal about 2 cups.

BASIC QUICHE

1 10-inch or 2 8-inch pie crusts,
   unbaked
1 tablespoon butter
1 medium onion, chopped or sliced
1-2 cups Swiss cheese (or Cheddar,
   Gruyere or mixed), grated

4 eggs, slightly beaten
2 cups milk (or half and half)
½ teaspoon salt
⅛ teaspoon pepper
Pinch of nutmeg

In a small saucepan, melt butter and sauté onion for 5 minutes. Bake pie crust 5 minutes at 450°. Cover with onions and cheese. In mixing bowl combine eggs, milk, salt, pepper and nutmeg. Mix well; pour over onions and cheese. Bake at 450° for 15 minutes. Reduce heat to 350° and bake another 30 minutes or until custard is well set. Remove from oven and let stand a few minutes before serving.

Favorite Variations:

(1.) **Quiche Lorraine:** Add 1½ to 2 cups of baked ham or Canadian bacon, diced.

(2.) **Vegetable Quiche:** Add 1 to 2 cups of your favorite vegetables that have been sautéed or slightly cooked, such as chopped spinach, sliced mushrooms, zucchini or tomatoes.

(3.) **Shrimp Quiche:** Add ½ pound of small cooked shrimp.

(4.) **Crab Quiche:** Add 1½ cups crabmeat. Season with an additional ½ teaspoon Worcestershire and substitute 1 tablespoon white wine for a tablespoon of the milk.

(5.) **Miniature Quiches:** Press small balls of pie crust in the bottoms and around sides of miniature muffin tins or tart molds. Bake unfilled shells at 400° for about 5 minutes until lightly browned. Fill with quiche filling. Bake another 15 minutes or until custard is set.

THREE-CHEESE MANICOTTI

1½ cups water	½ cup Parmesan cheese, grated
1 8-ounce can tomato sauce	2 eggs, beaten
1 1½-ounce package spaghetti	½ teaspoon salt
sauce mix	⅛ teaspoon pepper
2 cups shredded Mozzarella cheese	8 manicotti shells
1 cup Ricotta or small-curd cottage	
cheese	

Combine water, tomato sauce, and spaghetti sauce mix. Mix in a small saucepan. Simmer, uncovered, 10 minutes. Combine 1 cup Mozzarella cheese, Ricotta, Parmesan, eggs, salt, and pepper; stir gently and set aside. Cook manicotti shells according to package directions; drain. Stuff cheese mixture into manicotti shells, using about ¼ cup for each shell. Pour ½ cup sauce into a shallow 2-quart casserole; arrange manicotti shells in sauce, and pour remaining sauce over top. Sprinkle with remaining Mozzarella cheese. Bake, uncovered, at 350° for 25 to 30 minutes or until bubbly. Yield: 4 servings.

FAVORITE APPETIZER CHEESES

French Brie	Monterey Jack	Swiss
Boursin	Muenster	Gruyere
Camembert	Havarti	Dofino
Cheddar	Port du Salut	Kaukauna
Edam	Provolone	Port l'Évêque
Gouda	Roquefort (Blue)	

MEATS

FILET OF BEEF

1 whole beef tenderloin — about 6   A favorite marinade
    pounds

Trim fat from tenderloin. Marinate beef in a marinade (several choices follow) for several hours or overnight, turning several times. Preheat oven to 400°. Place tenderloin on rack of roasting pan (sprinkle with garlic salt), and lay the fat or strips of bacon at intervals over it. Put meat in oven and roast uncovered for 35-40 minutes for rare (140° on meat thermometer). Lower heat to 350°, and continue cooking for medium (cook a total of 1 hour or to 160° on thermometer) or well done (cook a total of 1 hour, 10 minutes or to 180° on thermometer).

Favorite Cooking Variation: Broil under preheated broiler 4 inches from the heat. Baste and turn frequently. Broil to preferred doneness — rare (25-30 minutes or to 140° on meat thermometer).

Note: 4 tenderloins thinly sliced will serve about 50 people for a cocktail party, depending on whether other meats are served. Always use a meat thermometer for accurate degree of doneness, since ovens cook at different degrees of heat.

Favorite Marinades:

  I. Mix 1 5-ounce bottle soy sauce; 1½ cups water; 4 tablespoons brown sugar; 1 tablespoon lemon juice; 1 tablespoon Worcestershire (optional); several cloves garlic, mashed; ½ box whole black peppers; and a dash of Accent. (This is a preservative; it tenderizes and adds flavor.)

 II. Marinate in 2 cups red wine, ½ teaspoon Dijon mustard, 1 tablespoon dried parsley, salt and pepper, 2 tablespoons mixed seasonings (Wham Sauce or mixed meat seasonings).

III. If you prefer not to marinate, rub tenderloin with ¾ teaspoon salt, ¼ teaspoon pepper, ⅛ teaspoon garlic salt, 2 teaspoons sugar, 1 teaspoon unseasoned meat tenderizer. Let stand 20 to 30 minutes. Lay pieces of fat over roast and cook using time chart above.

PARTY MUSTARD MOLD FOR BAKED HAM OR BEEF

1 envelope unflavored gelatin   ¼ teaspoon salt
½ cup cold water   ¼ teaspoon paprika
¼-½ cup mustard*   ½ cup heavy cream, whipped
1 cup mayonnaise

Soften gelatin in cold water. Stir over low heat until dissolved. Cool. Combine mustard, mayonnaise, salt and paprika. Add gelatin. Chill until thickened but not firm. Fold in whipped cream. Pour into a 1-quart oiled mold. Serve with ham or cold cuts. *Experiment with different mustards.

LONDON BROIL

1 large round steak, cut 1½ to 2
   inches thick
1 cup olive oil
¼ cup lemon juice
¼ cup vinegar
1 bay leaf, crushed

1 clove garlic, crushed
1 medium onion, sliced thin
½ teaspoon dried oregano leaves
1 teaspoon salt
½ teaspoon pepper

For marinade: combine oil, juice, vinegar, bay leaf, garlic, onion, oregano, salt and pepper in a jar and shake. Place meat in large baking dish. Pour marinade over it and cover. Let stand at room temperature for at least 4 hours, turning occasionally. (May leave overnight.) Drain and retain marinade to use again. To broil in electric fry pan, sprinkle pan with salt and brown meat 5 minutes on each side at 375°. Reduce heat to 225° and cook 6 minutes (rare) or 10 minutes (medium). To broil in oven, preheat broiler and cook 5 minutes on each side, brushing with marinade after turning. If a greater degree of doneness is desired, continue broiling. Carve by slicing thin slices on a diagonal, across the grain. Serves 4 to 6. (This is also delicious broiled on the grill.)

BEEF SUKIYAKI

2 tablespoons butter
1½ pounds sirloin steak (cut into
   small cubes)
1 cup green onions (sliced)
⅓ cup cooking sherry
1 cup mushrooms, sliced
2 cups bamboo shoots
1 cup celery (sliced into thin 1-inch
   strips)

½ cup green pepper (sliced into thin
   1-inch strips)
¼ cup beef broth or consommé
¼ cup soy sauce
2 tablespoons sugar
1 cup blanched almonds
Salt and pepper to taste
1 cup rice, cooked

Melt butter in skillet and sauté cubes of sirloin steak. When steak cubes are browned, add onions, wine, mushrooms, bamboo shoots, celery, green pepper, beef stock, soy sauce, sugar, almonds, and salt and pepper. Cover skillet and simmer for about 6 minutes. The items in this recipe should not be overcooked but should remain crisp and crunchy. Serve on a platter over a bed of cooked rice. Serves 6 to 8.

BEEF STROGANOFF

2 pounds lean round steak
Salt, pepper and flour
3 small onions, chopped
2 tablespoons butter
2 tablespoons tomato paste

1 10½-ounce can consommé or beef
   stock
Soy sauce to taste
2 cups sour cream
½ pound fresh mushrooms or 1
   large can, drained

Have beef cut in slices, less than ¼ inch thick. Pound in flour, salt and pepper. Cut into strips about 3 inches by ½ inch. Sauté onions in butter until just soft and yellow. Then add meat and sauté until well seared. Add tomato paste and enough consommé or beef stock to just cover. Add soy sauce to taste. Simmer until tender. Allow to cool to avoid curdling. Transfer to top of double boiler and add sour cream and mushrooms. Reheat in double boiler when ready to serve. Serve on rice. Serves 6.

BEST BARBECUED BEEF

2 pounds ground beef
1 onion, chopped
1 cup celery, chopped
1 12-ounce bottle chili sauce
1 cup catsup or more
2-3 tablespoons vinegar
3 tablespoons Worcestershire

1 tablespoon dry mustard
1 tablespoon brown sugar
1 teaspoon Morton's Nature
   Seasoning (optional)
Few drops Tabasco (optional)
Salt, pepper, paprika to taste

Brown beef, drain. Combine with remaining ingredients. Bake, covered, at 250° for 2 hours. Stir occasionally. Adjust seasonings. If dry, add more catsup. Serve with hamburger buns and with slaw. Flavor improves if made a day ahead. Freezes well. This may also be made on top of the stove. Makes about 12 sandwiches. A teenage favorite!!

DIVINE CASSEROLE

1 16-ounce package small egg
   noodles
2 10-ounce packages frozen
   spinach
2 pounds ground chuck
2 6-ounce cans tomato paste
2 teaspoons Worcestershire
Few drops Tabasco
Salt to taste

½ teaspoon oregano leaves
1 12-ounce carton creamed cottage
   cheese
1 8-ounce package cream cheese,
   softened
1 8-ounce carton sour cream
2 onions, chopped
2 sticks butter, melted
1 cup sharp Cheddar cheese, grated

Boil noodles by package directions; drain and rinse under hot water. Cook spinach according to package directions and drain. Brown meat and drain. Add tomato paste, Worcestershire, Tabasco, salt and oregano to meat. Mix well. Mix cottage cheese, cream cheese, sour cream and onions. Grease 2 2-quart casseroles. Layer ingredients in casserole in following order: noodles, butter, cheese mixture, spinach, noodles, butter and meat layer on top. Sprinkle ½ cup grated cheese on each casserole. Bake at 350° for 40 minutes or until bubbly. Freezes well. Serves 10-12.

GOLD MEDAL LASAGNE
Meat Sauce

1-1½ pounds ground chuck
1 garlic clove, minced
1 tablespoon parsley flakes
1 tablespoon basil flakes

1½ teaspoons salt
6 cups tomatoes (1 large and 1
   small can, drained)
2 6-ounce cans tomato paste

Cottage Cheese Mixture

1 8-ounce carton creamed cottage
   cheese
2 eggs, beaten
2 teaspoons salt
1 8-ounce box lasagne noodles

2 tablespoons parsley flakes
½ cup Parmesan cheese
½ teaspoon pepper
1 pound Mozzarella cheese, sliced

Cook noodles as directed on box. Drain. Brown meat; add other sauce ingredients and simmer 45 minutes to 1 hour. Grease bottom of a 2-quart rectangular baking casserole dish.* Put 3 noodles in lengthwise. Combine all cottage cheese mixture ingredients. Cover noodles with ½ the cheese mixture, ½ the Mozzarella cheese (save 2 slices to put on top) and ½ the meat mixture. Repeat procedure once, ending with meat on top. Cover with slices of Mozzarella cheese. Bake at 375° for 30 minutes. Serves 8.

*Note: This recipe fills casserole to the absolute top, so fill a small side casserole dish also, if desired.

Favorite Variation: To meat sauce add: 1 small can mushroom pieces, drained; 2 stalks celery and ½ green pepper, chopped.

MEAL-IN-A-LOAF MEATLOAF

4 pounds lean ground beef	1 8-ounce package Pepperidge
2 eggs	Farm Herb Stuffing
2 teaspoons salt	1 large onion, chopped
1 14-ounce jar pizza sauce	4 medium carrots, grated
1 6-ounce can tomato paste	4 stalks celery, chopped
	1 bottle Kitchen Bouquet

In a large bowl whisk eggs. Add salt, pizza sauce, tomato sauce and dry stuffing mix. Let stand until the stuffing has absorbed the sauce. Add all other ingredients except Kitchen Bouquet. Mix with hands until all ingredients are evenly distributed. Form into 4 loaves. Using pastry brush, cover each loaf generously with Kitchen Bouquet. At this point they may be frozen if desired. When ready to use, thaw and bake at 350° for 1 hour.

Favorite Variations: (1) May also be baked in muffin tins for individual servings but reduce the baking time to 30 minutes. (2) Catsup or an undiluted can of mushroom soup may be used as topping instead of Kitchen Bouquet. (3) Substitute 2 cups crushed saltine crackers for stuffing.

TACO PIE

1 pound ground beef	1 tablespoon chili powder
2 jalapeno peppers (hot), seeded	¼ teaspoon basil leaves
and chopped	⅛ teaspoon garlic powder
1 teaspoon salt	8 ounces sharp Cheddar cheese,
¼ teaspoon pepper	grated
1 15-ounce can tomatoes	1 8½-ounce box corn muffin mix
1 cup water	

Remove the seeds and chop the jalapeno peppers very fine. (For a milder dish, a 4-ounce can of chopped Mexican green chilies may be substituted for the peppers.) Brown beef with peppers, salt and pepper. Drain. Add tomatoes, water, chili powder, basil and garlic powder. Cook for about 10 minutes. Put into a greased 9 x 13-inch baking dish. Sprinkle cheese on top. Top with cornbread mix that has been made according to package directions. Bake at 475° for 15 minutes. Serves 8. To freeze this dish, do so before adding the cheese and corn muffin mix. Remove from the freezer, thaw and heat until warm (about 20 minutes) at 350°. Then add cheese and corn muffin mix and bake at 475° for 15 minutes more.

HOW TO BAKE A HAM

Smithfield or Country Ham:

To prepare: Place ham in a covered roaster, large enough to hold entire ham; add enough cold water to cover. Soak at least 12 hours; for less salty flavor, soak 24 hours, changing water at the end of first 12 hours.

After soaking, remove the ham from the water and discard water. Scrub ham to remove mold and pepper. Return ham to pot, add water to cover, and bring to a boil over high heat. Reduce heat, cover and barely simmer (approximately 20 to 30 minutes per pound, or until bone at end feels loose to touch) until done. Check occasionally while cooking, and add water to keep it covered.

To glaze: When done, remove ham from liquid and place on a rack, fat side up. Allow to cool 15 to 20 minutes. Remove skin and all but ¼ inch of the fat. Score the ham in a diamond pattern, putting a clove in the center of each diamond. Apply glaze by brushing with prepared glaze over entire surface (see Ham Glazes). Bake 30 minutes at 375°, basting several times with glaze. Allow to cool before carving.

Baked Mild-Cured Ham: Place ham on rack in shallow roasting pan, fat side up, and bake at 325°. Meat thermometer will register 150° when ham is done. Thirty minutes before ham is ready, apply glaze on scored surface. Baste several times with glaze. Cool before carving.

Ham	Bake
5 pound ham (½)	2½ hours
8 pound boned ham	3 hours
9-12 pound ham	3½ hours
15-20 pound boned ham	4 hours

Canned Ham: Bake an hour at 350°, basting several times with glaze. For cocktail party, take back to butcher and have it "shaved" or very thinly sliced.

Ham Glazes:

1. 1 cup brown sugar
   ¼ cup pineapple or orange juice
   1 teaspoon dry mustard
   Combine all ingredients.

2. 1 cup apricot preserves
   ½ cup honey
   1 tablespoon brandy
   1 tablespoon orange flavored liqueur
     or orange juice concentrate
   Combine all ingredients.

RAISIN SAUCE FOR HAM

2 tablespoons butter
2 tablespoons flour
1⅓ cups water
⅓ cup sugar
¼ teaspoon salt
⅓ cup orange juice
2 tablespoons vinegar

1-1½ cup raisins
¼ teaspoon cinnamon
¼ teaspoon grated lemon rind
  (optional)
1-3 teaspoons grated orange rind
  (optional)
5 cloves

Melt butter and add flour. Mix well and stir in remaining ingredients. Let simmer 10 minutes and stir several times. Serve warm with baked ham. Makes about 3 cups.

BARBECUE PORK

2 4 to 5 pound pieces fresh pork
   roast
½ cup Reunion Barbeque Sauce

Hickory smoked salt to taste
Salt, pepper and red pepper to taste

After placing meat on meat rack in heavy roasting pan with cover, rub the barbecue sauce into the meat, until meat is completely covered. If necessary, use more sauce. Cover, and put meat in 250° oven about 11:00 p.m. Remove from oven about 8:00 or 9:00 a.m. When cool, remove fat from meat, and chop into small pieces. Put in large bowl and season with seasonings. (It takes more than you think is needed.) When ready to serve, heat over low heat. Serve on toasted buns, or, as is, with heated barbecue sauce. Freezes well. Serves 14 to 16. Serve with slaw.

Reunion Barbeque Sauce: Mix ⅓ cup vinegar, ⅓ cup catsup, ¼ cup brown sugar, ¼ cup butter, 2 tablespoons Worcestershire, 2 tablespoons lemon juice, 2 teaspoons salt, 2 teaspoons paprika, 2 teaspoons chili powder, and 2 teaspoons dry mustard over low heat. Stir until butter is melted and brown sugar is dissolved. Good for chicken, pork or beef. Serves 10-12.

BRUNCH SAUSAGE RING

⅔ cup milk
1 egg
¾ cup rolled oats, uncooked
1½ pound pork sausage (good
   quality)
⅔ cup apples, peeled and chopped

¾ teaspoon salt
¾ teaspoon basil
½ teaspoon sage
6-8 peach halves
Parsley

Mix milk and egg. Add oats, sausage, apple, salt, basil, and sage and mix well. Place peaches, cavity side up, in the bottom of an ungreased 1½-quart ring mold. Pack sausage mixture firmly into mold. Bake for 1 hour at 350°. Pour off the grease. Invert on pan lined with several paper towels. Leave on towel for a few minutes until all grease has drained. Serve with additional cooked apples or scrambled eggs in the center. Garnish with apple wedges, additional peach halves or parsley. Serves 6.

SAUSAGE-RICE CASSEROLE

1 pound sausage
2 tablespoons butter
1 small onion, chopped
¼ green pepper, chopped
¼ cup celery, chopped
¾ cup fresh mushrooms, sliced
1 cup raw rice, uncooked

1 10-ounce can bouillon
1 soup can water
½ scant teaspoon thyme
1 teaspoon parsley
½ teaspoon salt
Pepper
⅓ cup blanched almonds

Brown sausage in frying pan. Remove and drain. Melt butter and sauté the onion, pepper and celery for 3 minutes. Add the mushrooms, cover and simmer 2 to 3 minutes. Put rice, sautéed vegetables, bouillon, water and seasonings in casserole, mixing them together. Cover and bake at 350° for 40 minutes. Remove from oven, and add the sausage and almonds, stirring thoroughly. Cook uncovered for 15 to 20 more minutes or until rice is tender.

CHICKEN BREASTS STUFFED WITH CHEESE

6 chicken breasts	1 10½-ounce can cream of chicken
Salt and pepper	soup, undiluted
½ cup butter, softened	¼ pound Mozzarella cheese
1 teaspoon marjoram	2 eggs, well beaten
½ teaspoon thyme	½ cup flour
2 tablespoons parsley, finely	½ cup dry white wine
chopped	¼ cup sliced almonds, toasted

Skin, debone and flatten chicken breasts. Sprinkle with salt and pepper; then spread with ¼ cup softened butter. Blend ¼ cup butter, marjoram, thyme, parsley and chicken soup. Cut Mozzarella cheese in 6 long strips and put one in center of each chicken breast. Roll and seal with toothpick. Dip in egg and roll breasts lightly in flour. Place in well-buttered baking dish and cover with soup mixture. Bake 40-45 minutes at 350°; then pour ½ cup dry white wine over chicken and cook 15-20 minutes more. Baste regularly with drippings. Top with almonds. Serves 6.

HERB CHICKEN

8 chicken breast halves, skinned	1 tablespoon oregano leaves
1 stick butter, melted	1 tablespoon parsley flakes
2 cups cornflake crumbs	1 teaspoon garlic powder
½ cup Parmesan cheese	1½ teaspoon salt
1 tablespoon rosemary leaves	1 teaspoon black pepper (optional)
1 tablespoon thyme leaves	

Roll chicken breasts in melted butter to coat. Mix next 9 ingredients together. Dip chicken in cornflake mixture to coat completely. Place in a shallow baking pan. Do not crowd pieces. Bake uncovered for 1 hour at 350°. Cornflake mixture may be stored in a sealed container in refrigerator. It makes a quick dish for a busy cook.

Favorite Variation: Chicken Nuggets: For party food, use this recipe with deboned chicken breasts, cut into strips.

TASTY CHICKEN BREASTS

8 chicken breasts (leave on wings)	1 cup sour cream
½ pound butter	2 tablespoons red currant jelly
4 tablespoons sherry	2 tablespoons Parmesan cheese
1 tablespoon tomato paste	1 4-ounce can mushrooms, sliced
2 tablespoons flour	Salt and pepper to taste
1 scant cup chicken stock (or 1	
bouillon cube and scant cup	
water)	

Cut tips of wings off but leave wings and breasts whole. Brown chicken in butter. As each piece browns, place in a 3-quart baking dish. Mix sherry, tomato paste, flour, chicken stock, sour cream, salt and pepper, and cook until thick. Add jelly and Parmesan cheese to sauce, mixing thoroughly, and pour over chicken breasts. Bake in 350° oven for 45 minutes to 1 hour or until tender. Baste often. Add drained mushrooms for last few minutes before serving. Serves 8. (Nice to serve over ham.)

COUNTRY CAPTAIN

2½ to 3 pound chicken, cut up or 8 chicken breasts*
¼ teaspoon pepper
¾ teaspoon salt
¼ teaspoon paprika
1 cup flour
½ cup cooking oil
1 tablespoon bacon grease or butter
2 green peppers, diced
1 large onion, chopped
2 tablespoons parsley, chopped
1 20-ounce can tomatoes
2 4-ounce cans mushrooms, drained
1 clove garlic, minced or 1/16 to ⅛ teaspoon garlic powder
1 teaspoon curry powder
1 teaspoon thyme
1 cup currants or raisins
1 cup almonds, blanched and browned but unsalted
1½ cups raw rice, cooked

Coat chicken in mixture of salt, pepper, paprika and flour. Fry in hot oil just until brown. Put aside. Pour oil out of pan and, into same frying pan, put bacon grease or butter and sauté slowly the green peppers, onions and parsley for about 10 to 15 minutes. Add tomatoes and cook about 10 minutes; then add mushrooms, herbs and seasonings to taste. Place chicken in a covered casserole or roaster, pour sauce over; cover and bake in 275° oven for 1½ to 2 hours (or 350° oven for 1 hour). Stir in currants and half the almonds 20 minutes before serving. Serve over hot fluffy rice. Sprinkle with remaining almonds. Serves 6 to 8.

*Chicken pieces in this recipe are usually left whole but may be deboned and chopped.

DIVINE CHICKEN DIVAN

6 large chicken breast halves
1 onion, chopped
1 celery stalk, chopped
1 carrot, chopped
½ bay leaf
2 10-ounce packages frozen broccoli spears
2 10½-ounce cans cream of chicken soup, undiluted
1 tablespoon lemon juice
1 cup Hellman's mayonnaise
1 8-ounce carton sour cream
1 cup sharp cheese, grated
1 teaspoon curry powder
Salt and pepper to taste
½ cup Parmesan cheese
Paprika
½ stick butter

Put chicken breasts in hot water to cover and simmer with onion, celery, carrot, bay leaf, salt and pepper for 1 hour or until meat is tender. Cook broccoli according to directions on package. Drain. Make sauce of chicken soup, lemon juice, mayonnaise, sour cream, grated cheese and seasonings. Spread broccoli spears on bottom of greased 3-quart baking dish. Sprinkle generously with Parmesan. Cut chicken up into bite size pieces and spread over broccoli. Sprinkle chicken with Parmesan. Pour sauce over entire casserole and sprinkle with Parmesan and paprika. Dot with butter. Cook 30 to 40 minutes in 350° oven or until hot and bubbly. Serves 6 to 8. Can be made ahead, refrigerated or frozen and cooked at time of serving.

Favorite Variation: Substitute turkey for chicken. Excellent use of leftover turkey! Another favorite topping is 1 package Pepperidge Farm Herb Seasoned Stuffing.

COMPANY CHICKEN AND CHIPPED BEEF

8 large chicken breast halves, boned and skinned
1 small jar chipped beef (enough to cover bottom of 9 x 13-inch baking dish)
8 strips of bacon
1 10-ounce can cream of mushroom soup, undiluted
1 4-ounce can mushrooms, drained
½ pint sour cream
½ cup milk
Paprika

Line baking dish with two layers of beef. Wrap a strip of bacon around each piece of chicken, and place in baking dish. Mix mushroom soup, mushrooms, sour cream, and milk, and pour over chicken. Bake in 325° oven for 1½ hours. Sprinkle with paprika. Do not add salt. Serves 8.

LEMON-TURKEY BAKE

4 cups turkey or chicken, cooked and diced
1 teaspoon lemon rind
1 teaspoon salt
1 teaspoon poultry seasoning
½ teaspoon lemon juice
⅛ teaspoon pepper
½ cup milk
2 cups Hellman's mayonnaise
2 cups sharp cheese, grated
3 cups celery, diced
4 boiled eggs, chopped
½ cup almonds or water chestnuts
1 onion, finely chopped
½ cup pimento, chopped
1 4-ounce can mushrooms, drained

In blender, mix lemon rind, salt, poultry seasoning, lemon juice, pepper, milk and mayonnaise. Then mix with rest of ingredients. Pour into 9 x 13-inch baking dish. Bake at 350° for 25-30 minutes. **Note:** A small turkey roast is just the right size for 4 cups. Serves 12.

Favorite Variations: (1) Cashews may be used instead of almonds, but add just before serving. (2) May top with 1 3-ounce can Chinese noodles or dry herb dressing. (3) Add 1 or 2 17-ounce cans tiny English peas (drained).

AFTER CHRISTMAS HAM AND TURKEY CASSEROLE

1 medium onion, chopped
2 tablespoons butter
3 tablespoons flour
½ teaspoon salt
Dash of pepper
1 4-ounce can mushrooms, sliced and drained
1 cup half and half cream or milk
2 tablespoons sherry
1 cup cooked ham, cubed
2 cups cooked turkey, cubed
½ 8-ounce can water chestnuts, sliced and drained
½ cup Swiss cheese, grated
3 tablespoons butter, melted
1½ cups bread crumbs

Sauté onion in butter until transparent. Stir in flour, salt and pepper. Add drained mushrooms, cream and sherry. Cook slowly, stirring until thickened. Add ham, turkey, and sliced water chestnuts. Mix thoroughly and pour into 1½ quart greased casserole. Top with grated cheese. Toss crumbs with melted butter and sprinkle on casserole. Bake in hot oven (400°) for 25 minutes or until brown. Serves 6.

ROAST TURKEY

Everyone has a "favorite" way to roast the Christmas turkey, but here is one that is hard to beat! (ATTENTION, NEW COOKS!! Don't forget to remove giblets and neck. Save to use in giblet gravy.) Wash the turkey thoroughly, including cavities, and check for pinfeathers. Pat dry. Sprinkle generously inside and out with salt and pepper.*

Place bird, breast side up, on a rack on roasting pan. Add 1 cup of water to bottom of pan. Rub the outside skin all over with 1 to 1½ sticks of softened butter. Place an aluminum tent over the bird, making tent large enough to cover loosely. Do not let foil touch heating unit. During cooking, lift foil tent, and baste several times with juice in bottom of pan. (Basting every 30 minutes assures a moist bird, so don't neglect!)

Roast in preheated 325° oven until tender; the drumstick will move easily when the turkey is done. Remove foil last 10 to 15 minutes to brown, if necessary.

(Cooking chart is for stuffed turkey. Reduce cooking time slightly if turkey is not stuffed.)

Turkey	Roast
4 to 6 pounds	3 to 4 hours
8 to 12 pounds	4 to 4½ hours
12 to 16	4½ to 5 hours
16 to 20	6 to 8 hours
20 to 24	8 to 9 hours

*If turkey is to be stuffed, fill the cavity with stuffing, but do not pack too tightly. Sew up the cavity or lace with skewers and tie legs to tail with string. Draw neck skin to back and secure with a toothpick or skewer. If turkey is not stuffed, place an onion and pieces of celery stalk inside cavity. Bake dressing in separate pan. (See Dressing recipes.)

Carving: Place bird on platter, breast up, and allow to cool 20 minutes or so for easy carving. Place before carver with bird's legs to his right. Secure bird with carving fork across breast bone, held firmly in the left hand. With carving knife in the right hand, cut leg away from body, cutting through joint next to bird. Then cut to separate joint of drumstick and second joint (thigh). Next, cut off wing. Breast meat can then be carved in thin slices. For a small family, carve one side completely, and save the other side for the second day. It remains moist if left on the bone, and this half also looks pretty on tray surrounded with fresh parsley if dinner is served buffet.

Basic Chicken or Turkey Gravy

1 tablespoon shortening	**¼ teaspoon pepper**
2 tablespoons flour	**2 cups chicken stock**
½ teaspoon salt	

Heat shortening, add flour and cook until brown. Add salt, pepper and stock. Stir constantly until thick. To eliminate "flour" taste, simmer over low heat for about 30 minutes. Stir to keep from sticking. Add more stock if needed.

Favorite Variation: Giblet Gravy: Cover turkey giblets with cold water; add ½ teaspoon salt and bring to a boil. Simmer until tender. Dice into small cubes. Add giblets and 1 chopped hard-boiled egg to Basic Turkey Gravy just before serving.

OLD-FASHIONED SOUTHERN CHICKEN
OR TURKEY DRESSING

4 cups cornbread, crumbled	Salt to taste
3 tablespoons celery, diced	½ teaspoon sage (optional)
1 small onion, minced	1 egg, well beaten
1 tablespoon poultry seasoning (optional)	2 tablespoons butter, melted
1 teaspoon parsley flakes	Enough hot chicken broth to moisten

Mix cornbread, celery, onion and seasonings. Add well-beaten egg and butter; mix thoroughly. Moisten with hot chicken broth until soft. Pour into a well-greased baking pan. Bake at 400° for 25-30 minutes or use to stuff a 10 to 14 pound turkey. (**Note:** If using to stuff turkey, keep dressing dry by adding very little broth. It will absorb additional moisture in the turkey. Pack loosely!)

QUICK AND EASY BASIC DRESSING

1 16-ounce package dry Pepperidge Farm Herb Seasoned Stuffing Mix	½ to 1 cup onion, chopped
	1 cup celery, diced
	1 egg, beaten
2 cups chicken broth	1½ sticks of butter, melted

Mix all ingredients thoroughly. Stuffs 12-14 pound turkey or bake in a lightly greased 9 x 13-inch pan for 30 minutes at 350°.

Favorite Variations for Either Dressing: (Note: When adding additional ingredients, it increases the quantity of dressing. Plan accordingly.)

Mushroom: Add 1 to 2 cups sliced mushrooms, drained, or fresh mushrooms, sautéed.

Virginia Oyster: Add ½ cup sautéed mushrooms, 2 tablespoons chopped, fresh parsley and 1 to 2 cups oysters (depending on your love of oysters), drained and cut in half.

Pecan: Add 1 cup chopped pecans.

Sausage:
  I. **Basic Sausage:** Add ½ pound hot sausage, cooked, drained and crumbled.
 II. **Apple-Sausage:** Add to above sausage: ½ cup green pepper, chopped, ½ cup pecans, chopped, and 2 tart apples, unpeeled, cored and cubed.
III. **For Sausage Lovers!:** Make "Quick and Easy Basic Dressing." Add 1 pound cooked and drained sausage, 1 cup sautéed mushrooms, ⅓ teaspoon thyme and 3 tablespoons fresh, chopped parsley. Stuff a 12-pound turkey or bake in a lightly greased 9 x 13 inch pan for 30 minutes at 350°.

Caution: When preparing dressing and turkey in advance, refrigerate separately and stuff just before cooking. Remove leftover dressing from turkey, cool immediately and refrigerate separately.

FAVORITE TURKEY TIPS

After cooking the turkey or a roast, let it stand for 10-15 minutes before carving.

Frozen meats retain their juices better if they are thawed in the refrigerator.

SEAFOOD

ROYAL SEAFOOD CASSEROLE

2 10½-ounce cans condensed cream of shrimp soup, undiluted
½ cup mayonnaise
1 small onion, grated
¾ cup milk
¼ teaspoon salt
Dash of white pepper
Dash of seasoned salt
Dash of ground nutmeg
Dash of cayenne pepper

3 pounds raw shrimp, boiled and cleaned
1 7½-ounce can crabmeat, drained
1 5-ounce can water chestnuts, drained and sliced
1½ cups celery, diced
3 tablespoons fresh parsley, minced
1⅓ cups raw rice, cooked
Paprika
Slivered almonds

Cook rice according to package directions. Blend soup with mayonnaise in a large bowl. Add onion, then milk. Now begin seasonings; use a heavy hand, because the rice is bland and so is the seafood. When mixture is well seasoned, combine with rice and other ingredients except paprika and almonds. Check seasoning; add a few tablespoons of milk if mixture seems dry; it should be moist. Turn into a large, shallow, buttered casserole; sprinkle with paprika and scatter almonds generously over top. Bake, uncovered, at 350° for about 30 minutes, or until hot and bubbly. Freezes well. Serves 10-12.

Favorite Variation: Add 1 small jar chopped pimento, drained; 1 large can button mushrooms, drained; 3 hard-boiled eggs, chopped; and/or 1 6-ounce can lobster. Additional ingredients may increase the number of servings.

UNIVERSITY LOW-COUNTRY BOIL

New potatoes, 4 per person
Hillshire Polish Sausage — ¼ pound per person
Corn on the cob — 1 or 2 half ears per person

Unpeeled headless green shrimp — ⅓ pound per person
Shrimp or seafood seasoning bag

Put potatoes in water to cover. Boil for 25 minutes. Add sausage, cut in 3″ sections, and cook 20 minutes. Lift potatoes and sausage out of water onto a pan on top of stove. Add corn to water and cook 7 to 10 minutes. Remove. Add a shrimp seasoning bag, simmer for 5 minutes, remove, and add shrimp to boiling water. Cook 3 more minutes or until done. Drain well. Spread on a large platter and top with potatoes, sausage, and corn on the cob. (Hot shrimp will reheat the rest.) **Note:** For an easy way to serve, cover the table with newspaper and let everyone peel his own shrimp. Supply melted butter, cocktail sauce and small individual paper plates for shrimp shells. Add a green salad for a complete meal. A blue-ribbon favorite of college students.

Favorite Easy Cooking Variation: Boil potatoes 20 minutes, add sausage and cook 10 more minutes. Add corn and cook 7 minutes, then add shrimp. Boil 3 more minutes and drain well. Everything is boiled together and no shrimp seasoning is added.

ALL-TIME FAVORITE SHRIMP WITH ARTICHOKES

1 20-ounce can artichoke hearts
¾ pound raw shrimp, boiled and
    cleaned
¼ pound fresh or canned
    mushrooms, sliced
5 tablespoons butter
¼ cup onions, chopped

4 tablespoons flour
1½ cups half and half
1 tablespoon Worcestershire
Salt and pepper to taste
3 tablespoons dry sherry
¼ cup grated Parmesan cheese
Paprika

Drain artichokes, slice in half and arrange in buttered 9 x 13 inch baking dish. Spread the cooked shrimp over these. Sauté mushrooms in butter for about 5 minutes, lift out and sprinkle over shrimp and artichokes. Cook onions in same butter until transparent. Add flour and cook a minute or two longer. Add half and half and stir until thickened. Add Worcestershire, salt (lightly, as Parmesan cheese is salty), pepper and sherry to cream sauce and pour over contents of baking dish. Sprinkle with Parmesan cheese and paprika. Bake at 375° for 20 minutes. Serves 6.

DEVILED CRAB

1 bell pepper, chopped
1 onion, chopped
1 garlic clove, mashed
2 stalks celery, chopped
*3 tablespoons fresh parsley,
    chopped
4 slices bread
½ cup water

½ cup sharp cheese, grated
3 6½-ounce cans crab meat, drained
⅓ cup mayonnaise
2 eggs, beaten
1 tablespoon Worcestershire
Juice of 1 lemon (2 tablespoons)
Add to taste: seasoned salt, pepper
    and Tabasco

Sauté bell pepper, onion, garlic, celery and parsley. Soak bread slices in water and squeeze out. Discard water. Mix everything together. Fill individual baking shells. Bake at 300° for 30-40 minutes. May be made the day before and kept covered in the refrigerator until ready to bake. Fills 8-10 shells. Fresh crab meat (1 pint) is a delicious substitute for the canned. *If using dried parsley, use only 1 tablespoon.

HAM AND CRABMEAT

1 cup crabmeat
A shake of Worcestershire
1 teaspoon pimento, chopped
1½ tablespoons mayonnaise

Tabasco (2 or 3 drops)
4 slices of baked ham
4 pineapple slices
½ cup cornflakes, crushed

Mix crabmeat, Worcestershire, pimento, mayonnaise, and Tabasco. Place ham slices in baking dish. Coat pineapple slices with crushed cornflakes and put one on top of each ham slice. Top each pineapple slice with ¼ of the crabmeat mixture. Bake at 350° for 15 minutes. Serves 4.

SCALLOPED OYSTERS

1 quart oysters
½ cup butter
2 tablespoons flour
Salt and pepper

2 tablespoons onion, finely chopped
1 tablespoon Worcestershire
2 tablespoons lemon juice
2 to 3 cups cracker crumbs

Drain oysters, reserving juice. Melt butter and add flour and enough oyster juice to make a roux. Pour in the oysters. Add next four remaining ingredients and stir. Layer in casserole ½ cracker crumbs, then oysters, and top with remaining cracker crumbs. Dot with butter. Bake at 450° for 20 minutes. Serves 8.

Favorite Variations: (1) Add 2 tablespoons green pepper and/or celery, chopped. (2) Substitute Pepperidge Farm Herb Stuffing Mix for crackers. Add a little milk if it needs it for moisture.

Seafood Shells: Crumble a few crackers to cover bottom of shells. Cover with oyster mixture and top with additional buttered cracker crumbs. Broil for 5 minutes or until browned.

SALMON LOAF

1 16-ounce can salmon	1 cup cracker or bread crumbs
1 tablespoon butter	1 10-ounce can cream of celery
1 tablespoon onion, grated	soup, undiluted
1 bell pepper, chopped	2 eggs, beaten

Mince salmon. Remove bones. Sauté onion and bell pepper in butter. Mix salmon, bread crumbs, ½ cup of the cream of celery soup, eggs, onion, butter and bell pepper. The rest of the soup is reserved to heat and serve as a sauce with the loaf. Bake in a small, greased loaf pan at 350° for 30 minutes. Remove from the pan and put on a baking sheet. Brown in the oven for a few minutes. Pour sauce over loaf and decorate with parsley.

TUNA CASSEROLE

1 10-ounce can cream of mushroom	1 cup celery, finely chopped
soup, undiluted	¼ cup onion, minced
1 6½-ounce can tuna fish, drained	Salt and pepper
¼ cup water or evaporated milk	½ cup cashew nuts, chopped
1 3-ounce can chow mein noodles	(optional)
	2 teaspoons soy sauce

Combine the above, using ½ of the noodles. Sprinkle remaining noodles over the top. Bake at 325° for 40 minutes in greased casserole. Serves 4.

VEGETABLES

SOUTHERN BAKED BEANS

1 small onion, minced	4 tablespoons catsup
½ bell pepper, chopped	2 tablespoons molasses
2 stalks celery, chopped	2 tablespoons brown sugar
2 tablespoons bacon drippings or	3 drops Tabasco sauce
butter	Salt to taste
1 20-ounce can pork and beans	3 slices bacon, uncooked

Sauté onion, bell pepper, and celery in bacon drippings. Mix all ingredients except bacon. Put in a greased shallow baking dish. Cut bacon slices in half and put on top of beans. Bake at 375° for 30 minutes. Serves 4 generously.

BROCCOLI AND/OR CAULIFLOWER CASSEROLE

1 10-ounce package frozen chopped broccoli
1 10-ounce package frozen cauliflower
1 teaspoon garlic salt
1 10-ounce can mushroom soup, undiluted

1 egg, beaten
1½ cups sharp Cheddar cheese, grated
1 cup Pepperidge Farm Stuffing
½ stick butter, melted

Cook broccoli and cauliflower a few minutes, adding garlic salt to the cooking water. Drain vegetables. Add soup, egg and cheese. Put in a greased 2-quart casserole and top with mixture of stuffing tossed with melted butter. Bake at 350° for 30 minutes.

Favorite Variations: (1) Top instead with can of fried onion rings or Ritz cracker crumbs. (2) For a heavier, more filling casserole, add 2 cups cooked rice that has been cooked in the broccoli and cauliflower stock. (3) Add 2 cups of cooked chicken for a flavorful main dish. (4) Use 2 packages of broccoli and no cauliflower. (5) Add ½ cup chopped celery, ½ cup sliced mushrooms and 1 small chopped onion that has been sautéed in 2 tablespoons butter.

FRENCH STYLE GREEN BEAN CASSEROLE

3 10-ounce packages frozen French style green beans
1 10½-ounce can mushroom soup, undiluted
1 10½-ounce can cream of chicken soup, undiluted

1 cup sharp cheese, grated
1 5-ounce can water chestnuts, drained and sliced
1 8-ounce can bean sprouts, drained
1 2.8 ounce-can French-fried onion rings

Mix first six ingredients and bake in greased casserole in 350° oven for 30 minutes. Top with French-fried onions and brown 10 minutes more.

CARROT RING

¾ cup butter, softened
½ cup (scant) brown sugar
1 teaspoon baking powder
1 teaspoon soda
½ teaspoon salt

1¼ cups flour
1 egg, beaten
1 cup carrots, grated and packed
1 tablespoon water
1 teaspoon lemon juice

Cream butter and brown sugar. Mix dry ingredients, then add them and all other ingredients to sugar and butter mixture. Spoon into a well-greased 9-inch ring mold. Place in a pan of hot water (at least halfway up sides of mold). Bake for 45 minutes at 350°. It will be slightly brown when ready. Take out of pan of water and let stand 5 minutes. Loosen mold with a knife and turn out on a platter. Either serve plain or with another vegetable in the center — a contrasting color is pretty. This is just as good warmed over!

● **Herb Rule:** Use 2 or 3 times as much fresh herbs as dried . . . taste to be sure!

CORN PUDDING

¼ cup butter
¼ cup flour
1 teaspoon salt
1½ tablespoons sugar

1¾ cup milk
3 cups fresh or frozen corn (or 2 cans, drained)
3 eggs, beaten

Melt butter; stir in flour, salt and sugar. Cook until bubbly. Add milk and cook until thick. Stir in corn; then, add beaten eggs. Pour into well-greased oven dish, and bake in a pan of hot water at 350° for 45 minutes.

SWEET POTATO SOUFFLE

1 29-ounce can sweet potatoes, mashed
1 cup sugar
6 tablespoons butter, softened
1 teaspoon salt
1 teaspoon vanilla

2 eggs, beaten
1 cup pecans, broken
¾ stick butter, softened
½ cup brown sugar
¾ cup cornflakes, crushed

Beat together drained and mashed potatoes, sugar, 6 tablespoons butter, salt, vanilla and eggs. Put in buttered 2-quart casserole dish. Make topping by mixing pecans, ¾ stick butter, brown sugar and crushed cornflakes. (Measure cornflakes **after** they are crushed.) Mix and put on top of sweet potato mixture. Bake at 350° for 45 minutes. Serves 6-8. This is very sweet and a favorite with pork dishes.

Favorite Variations: (1) Add ½ cup raisins or ½ cup coconut. (2) Make it more spicy with ½ teaspoon ground cloves, 1½ teaspoons allspice and 1½ teaspoons cinnamon. (3) To put in orange shells (after scooping the orange out to use in ambrosia), eliminate eggs. Add ½ cup orange juice and one teaspoon of apple pie spice. Mix thoroughly. Substitute marshmallows for cornflake topping. Fill shells and top with miniature marshmallows. Bake at 350° for 15 to 20 minutes.

POTATO-MUSHROOM CASSEROLE

8 or 9 boiling potatoes
½ cup butter
2 medium onions, chopped
2 3-ounce cans mushrooms, sliced, drained

Salt and pepper
⅓ cup hot milk
1 cup sour cream
Paprika

Peel and boil potatoes. While they cook, melt butter in skillet and sauté onions slowly until yellow. Add drained mushrooms. Sauté about 2 minutes. Remove onions and mushrooms; set aside, leaving the butter in the skillet. When potatoes are done, drain and whip lightly. Add seasonings and just enough hot milk to make consistency of mashed potatoes. Beat in the butter left in the skillet. Spread a thin layer of potatoes in shallow 2-quart rectangular baking dish. Cover with a thin layer of sautéed onions and mushrooms, then a layer of sour cream. Repeat. Top with potatoes. Brush top with a little melted butter. Sprinkle with paprika and bake at 350° for 20 or 30 minutes until lightly browned. This may be made ahead of time. Any left over can be frozen. Serves 8 to 10.

HASH BROWN POTATO CASSEROLE

1 32-ounce package frozen hash
　brown potatoes, thawed
¾ cup butter, melted
½ cup onion, chopped

1 10½-ounce can cream of chicken
　soup, undiluted
1 8-ounce carton sour cream
1 cup sharp Cheddar cheese, grated
2 cups cornflakes, crushed

Combine potatoes, ½ cup butter, onion, soup, sour cream and cheese. Stir well. Pour into a greased 2½-quart casserole. Toss crushed cereal with the remaining ¼ cup butter. Sprinkle over potato mixture. Bake at 350° for 50 minutes. Serves 10-12. Good for brunch, breakfast or dinner.

RICE FAVORITES

In all sections of the country, rice is a holiday favorite. Here are some favorite things to do with rice.

SIMPLY RICE: In a 1½ or 2-quart casserole, stir together 1 cup raw converted rice, 1 10½-ounce can beef consommé, undiluted; 1 10½-ounce can onion soup with beef stock, undiluted; and 1 4-ounce can sliced mushrooms, drained. Bake covered at 350° for 1 hour. Serves 6. So simple, so good, and needs no gravy.

NUTTED-ORANGE RICE: Sauté a small chopped onion in 4 tablespoons butter and 1 teaspoon salt. Cook 1 cup raw rice with 1¾ cup chicken stock, ¼ cup orange juice, grated rind of 1 orange and sautéed onion and butter. When rice is done, toss with ½ cup golden raisins, ½ cup chopped walnuts or pecans and orange sections (cut in half) of 1 orange. Serve in orange shells. (¼ teaspoon each of thyme and cinnamon is a tasty option.)

PARTY RICE RING: Cook 2 cups raw rice according to package or recipe directions. Pack into a well-greased 1½-quart ring mold. Set in a pan of hot water; cover and steam for about 60 minutes until the rice is hot. Unmold on a heated platter and fill center with a green vegetable. Rice with chopped parsley is especially pretty in a mold.

REHEATING RICE: To reheat or keep rice hot, use a steamer or steam rice in a colander over boiling water.

HOPPIN JOHN

1 cup raw rice
4 slices bacon
1 medium onion, chopped
2½ cups water

1 teaspoon salt
15-ounce can black-eyed peas,
　drained

Fry bacon, remove from pan and crumble. Sauté onion in bacon grease. Bring water to a boil. Add onion, bacon grease, salt and rice to boiling water. Cover tightly; lower temperature and simmer for 20 minutes. Add bacon and black-eyed peas. Simmer 5 more minutes. Remove from heat and let stand about 5 minutes until liquid is absorbed. Serves 8.

South Carolina was the birthplace of rice in America. Many rice recipes and traditions have been passed from generation to generation and are still enjoyed across the Carolinas today. "Hoppin John" is believed to bring good luck if eaten on New Year's Day. Complete the meal with collard greens (for wealth) and ham hock (for health) — a guaranteed HAPPY NEW YEAR!

WILD RICE CASSEROLE

1 cup raw wild rice or a wild rice blend	1 10½-ounce can cream of mushroom soup, undiluted
3 cups water	¾ cup half and half cream
1 teaspoon salt	¼ teaspoon marjoram
2 tablespoons butter	⅛ teaspoon basil
4 tablespoons onion, minced	⅛ teaspoon tarragon
2 tablespoons green pepper, chopped	½ teaspoon curry powder
1 4-ounce can sliced mushrooms, drained	½ teaspoon salt
	¼ teaspoon pepper

Cook rice according to package directions using the 1 teaspoon salt in the 3 cups water. While rice is cooking, in another pan melt butter and sauté the onion, green pepper and mushrooms for about 5 minutes. Stir in the mushroom soup, cream and spices. Heat the mixture **slowly** for about 10 minutes. When wild rice is ready, rinse it in a colander and add the rice to the cream sauce mixture. Pour into a greased 2-quart casserole and bake at 350° for 20-30 minutes until heated thoroughly. This is better made the day before so herbs can blend, but baking time will need to be increased since ingredients are not already hot. Serves 8. **Note:** 6 to 8 whole, medium size, fresh mushrooms that have been greased with butter make a lovely garnish. Place them on the casserole the last 8 minutes of cooking time, **not before.** Decorate with parsley sprigs just before serving.

Favorite Variation: 2 cups shrimp, crab or chicken may be added for an elegant main dish. This will increase the number of people served.

ROYAL SPINACH AND ARTICHOKE

1 8½-ounce can artichoke hearts, drained	Salt and pepper to taste
1 8-ounce can water chestnuts, sliced	1 teaspoon lemon juice
1 8-ounce package cream cheese	3 10-ounce packages frozen chopped spinach, cooked and drained
1 stick butter	Seasoned bread crumbs or cracker crumbs
¼ teaspoon garlic powder (optional)	

Cut artichoke hearts in half and place in buttered casserole. Add water chestnuts. Mix cream cheese and butter together in the top of a double boiler. When they have melted, stir to blend well and add garlic, salt, pepper, lemon juice and spinach. Pour over artichokes and water chestnuts. Bake at 350° for 30 minutes. Sprinkle top with seasoned bread crumbs or crushed Ritz crackers. Bake a few more minutes until they are toasted. Serves 6-8.

CANS-CAN-BE-GOOD VEGETABLE CASSEROLE

1 16-ounce can Veg-All Mixed Vegetables, drained	½ cup sharp Cheddar cheese, grated
¼ cup water chestnuts, sliced	½ cup mayonnaise
¼ cup onion, chopped	1 tablespoon butter, melted
½ cup celery, chopped	½ cup Ritz cracker crumbs

Mix all ingredients except butter and cracker crumbs. Combine butter and cracker crumbs and sprinkle on top. Bake at 325° for about 25 minutes. Serves 4.

SQUASH SOUFFLE

8 squash, diced	3 tablespoons butter
1 large onion, chopped	3 tablespoons flour
3 cups water	½ teaspoon salt
1 teaspoon salt	½ cup Cheddar cheese, grated
1 teaspoon sugar	2 eggs, slightly beaten
1 teaspoon pepper	12 Ritz crackers, crumbled
1½ cups milk	1 large carrot, grated (optional)

Cook squash and onion in water with 1 teaspoon salt, sugar and pepper, until vegetables are done. Make a cream sauce of milk, butter, flour and ½ teaspoon salt. Add cheese, stirring until melted. Butter a 2-quart casserole. Drain squash in colander, then mash squash through colander into a bowl placed under colander. Mix cream sauce with squash; add carrots and eggs. Pour into casserole. Top with cracker crumbs. Bake at 350° for 30 minutes. Serves 6-8.

DELUXE SCALLOPED TOMATOES

7 fresh tomatoes	½ teaspoon salt
½ cup butter, melted	½ teaspoon nutmeg
1 cup onion, chopped	3 cups white bread cubes
2 tablespoons brown sugar	

Peel tomatoes, cut 3 slices to reserve for top garnish, and chop rest of tomatoes. Sauté onion in 2 tablespoons of the butter. Add all remaining ingredients to onions, except bread cubes and remaining butter. Simmer for 15 minutes. Toss bread with butter to coat. Layer 2 cups bread cubes in a greased 10-inch quiche or pie pan. Cover with tomato mixture and top with remaining bread. Bake at 375° **covered** for 15 minutes. Uncover, top with reserved tomato slices brushed lightly with vegetable oil and bake **uncovered** for 15 more minutes. Serves 8.

Favorite Winter Variation: Substitute 3½ cups canned tomatoes for fresh tomatoes. Garnish with parsley.

ZUCCHINI SOUFFLE

3 cups zucchini, unpeeled and grated	½ cup cooking oil
	½ teaspoon seasoned salt
½ onion, thinly sliced	½ teaspoon regular salt
2 tablespoons parsley, chopped	½ cup Parmesan cheese
1 garlic clove, pressed	4 eggs, lightly beaten
1 cup Bisquick biscuit mix	1 tablespoon butter, melted

Mix everything but eggs and melted butter. Add eggs last. Put in greased 9 x 13-inch baking dish. Drizzle with melted butter. Bake 35 minutes at 350°. Cut in squares to serve.

Favorite Variation: Cut into small squares and use as appetizers. Great!!

- A pinch of sugar in the water when cooking vegetables improves the flavor. Use a pinch of baking soda in green vegetables to bring out the flavor. A bouillon cube in green beans, butter beans and leafy green vegetables enhances the flavor.
- Instant mashed potatoes are great for thickening gravies, stews and sauces and will not lump.

BAKED BANANAS-CRANBERRY SAUCE CASSEROLE

4 bananas
1 cup whole-berry cranberry sauce
¼ cup brown sugar
Pinch of salt

3 tablespoons dry sherry
2 tablespoons butter, melted
2 tablespoons slivered almonds,
roasted (optional)

Mix cranberry sauce, sugar, salt and sherry. Peel bananas, slice lengthways, and arrange in shallow greased baking dish. Brush with butter. Spoon cranberry sauce mix over bananas. Bake at 350° for 15 to 20 minutes, basting at least once. Sprinkle with almonds before serving. Serves 4.

CRANBERRY-APPLE TREAT

1 cup sugar
3 cups unpeeled apples, chopped
2 cups fresh cranberries
1½ cups rolled oats, uncooked

½ cup brown sugar
¼ cup pecans, chopped
1 stick butter, melted

Mix 1 cup sugar, apples and cranberries. Put in 9 x 9-inch baking dish. In separate bowl, mix oats, brown sugar, nuts and melted butter to make topping. Put topping on apple mixture. Bake at 350° for 45 minutes. Serves 8.

WINTER CURRIED FRUIT

⅓ cup butter
¾ cup brown sugar, packed
3 teaspoons curry powder
1 24-ounce can pear halves

½ cup blanched almonds
½ cup cherries
1 24-ounce can apricots or peaches
1 11-ounce can pineapple chunks

Heat oven to 325°. Melt butter, add brown sugar and curry. Drain and dry fruits. Place in casserole and pour the butter mix over the mixed fruits. Bake 1 hour. Serve immediately or cool, refrigerate, and reheat 20 minutes at 325° when ready to serve. Serves 12.

APPLE CHART

Best All-Purpose Cooking Apples: Courtland, Golden Delicious, Granny Smith, Jonathan, McIntosh, Newtown Pippin, Rome Beauty

Best Apples for Baking Whole: Courtland, Golden Delicious, Newtown Pippin, Winesap

Best Eating Apples: Courtland, Red Delicious, Golden Delicious, Empire, Granny Smith, Jonathan, Macoun, McIntosh, Winesap

Hint: A little Calvados or Applejack adds extra flavor to apple dishes.

BREADS

CHEESE PUFFS

¼ pound sharp Cheddar cheese	1 stick butter
1 3-ounce package cream cheese	3 egg whites, beaten
	*Loaf of unsliced bread

Melt cheeses and butter in double boiler. Cool. Fold in egg whites that have been beaten until stiff peaks form. Cut bread into 2-inch cubes and coat with cheese mixture. Place on greased cookie sheet and refrigerate overnight. When ready to use, bake 10-12 minutes at 400°. Before these have been baked they may be frozen on the cookie sheet, then removed and stored in a plastic bag in freezer until ready to use. These are especially good with soup or salad meals.
*Leftover French bread may also be used.

COLONIAL CHEESE BISCUITS

½ pound sharp Cheddar cheese	½ teaspoon salt
2 sticks butter, softened	½ teaspoon paprika
2 cups plus 2 tablespoons flour	Confectioners sugar

Leave cheese out overnight and cream it like butter. Beat in butter. Add flour, salt and paprika. Mix well and drop by teaspoonsful on a greased cookie sheet. Bake at 450° for 8 minutes. Sprinkle with confectioners sugar while still hot. These may also be baked in miniature muffin pans but increase the baking time to 13 minutes. Serve hot. These freeze well and are good as appetizers or served with the meal.

SERENDIPITY ROLLS

1½ sticks butter, melted	¼ cup sugar
1 package dry yeast	1 egg, beaten
2 cups warm water	4 cups self-rising flour

Melt butter and cool to room temperature. Dissolve yeast in water. Cream sugar with butter in large bowl and add egg. Add yeast and mix in flour. Place in airtight glass or plastic container and store in refrigerator until ready to use. This mixture may be used immediately or stored for 3-4 days in refrigerator. When ready to use, drop by spoonfuls into greased muffin tins. Bake 15-20 minutes at 425°. Makes 2 dozen.

MAKE-AHEAD FREEZER BISCUITS

5 cups flour	1 cup shortening
¼ cup sugar	1 package yeast
3 teaspoons baking powder	2 tablespoons warm water
1 teaspoon soda	2 cups buttermilk (room
1 teaspoon salt	temperature)

Sift dry ingredients together. Cut in shortening. Dissolve yeast in warm water and add to buttermilk. Add liquid mixture to dry ingredients. Turn out on lightly floured board and roll and cut. Place on baking sheet. Bake immediately or freeze on baking sheet before baking. After biscuits are frozen, store in freezer bags. When ready to use, take out about 30 minutes before baking time. Dip in melted butter and place on baking sheet. Bake at 400° for 12-15 minutes. This amount makes enough for a family of 4 or 5 for 6 meals.

Party Biscuits: Roll out biscuit dough on floured surface. With a knife, cut into small squares. This is much quicker and more interesting than the traditional round ones.

SALLY LUNN

1 package dry yeast	3 eggs
½ cup warm water	4 cups flour
½ cup Crisco shortening	1 teaspoon salt
½ cup soft butter	1 cup milk
½ cup sugar	

All ingredients and mixing bowl should be room temperature!!
Soften yeast in warm water. Cream shortening, butter and sugar. Beat in eggs. Add half the flour and all the salt. Stir in milk and yeast mixture. Add remaining flour and beat well. Cover and let rise in a warm place until double in size (about 2 hours). Beat down the batter; then spoon into greased tube or bundt pan. Cover and let rise again until doubled (about 1 hour). Watch this rising carefully because you do not want it to over-rise. Preheat oven to 325° and bake at this temperature for 20 minutes. Increase temperature to 375° and bake 25 more minutes. Total baking time will be 45 minutes. This may be baked ahead and frozen. To reheat, thaw and wrap tightly in aluminum foil. Heat at 300° for about 20-30 minutes. Cut at the table and pass melted butter.

Early Virginia settlers brought this recipe from England. According to legend, an English girl sold this bread on the streets of London. She called it "Sol et Lune" which is French for sun and moon. The top of the bread was golden like the sun and the bottom white like the moon. The bread became known as "Sally Lunn."

POPPY SEED BREAD

1½ cups sugar	2 eggs
¼ cup poppy seeds	¾ cup cooking oil
2 cups flour	1 teaspoon vanilla
1 teaspoon baking powder	1 cup evaporated milk
1 teaspoon salt	

Mix dry ingredients and poppy seeds; then add liquid ingredients. Mix well. Bake at 350° for 1 hour in well-greased 9 x 5-inch loaf pan. Excellent as miniature sandwiches made with cream cheese that has been softened and mixed with a little milk or orange juice.

PUMPKIN BREAD

3⅓ cups flour	3 teaspoons cinnamon
3 cups sugar	1 cup cooking oil
2 teaspoons soda	⅔ cup water or orange juice
1½ teaspoons salt	1 can (2 cups) pumpkin
3 teaspoons nutmeg	4 eggs

Mix dry ingredients, then add other ingredients. Beat until smooth. Bake in 2 greased 9 x 5-inch loaf pans or in one tube pan. Bake for one hour at 350°. May need to bake a little longer if baked in a tube pan.

CREAM CHEESE BRAID BREAD

1 cup sour cream	½ cup warm water
1 teaspoon salt	2 packages yeast
½ cup sugar	2 eggs
1 stick butter	4 cups flour

Cream Cheese Filling

1 pound cream cheese	⅛ teaspoon salt
¾ cup sugar	2 teaspoons vanilla

Glaze

2 cups confectioners sugar	4 tablespoons milk
2 teaspoons vanilla	

Scald sour cream. Add salt, sugar and butter. Cool to lukewarm and be sure butter is melted. Measure warm water in large warm bowl. Sprinkle with yeast and stir. Add sour cream mixture, eggs and flour. Mix well, cover and refrigerate overnight. Next day, divide dough into 4 pieces. Roll each piece into a rectangle about 8 x 12 inches. Mix filling ingredients and spread generously over rectangles. Keep filling away from edges. Roll up each like a jelly roll. Pinch ends together and fold under slightly. Place on greased aluminum foil on a baking sheet. With scissors, cut each roll deeply, making cuts alternating from side to side to resemble a braid. Let rise until double in bulk, about 2 hours. Bake at 375° for 12-15 minutes. While hot, spread with glaze mixture. Makes 4 loaves.

SOUR CREAM COFFEE CAKE

4 tablespoons brown sugar	2 cups flour
2 teaspoons cinnamon	1½ teaspoons baking powder
1 cup pecans, chopped	½ teaspoon baking soda
1 cup real butter	1 cup sour cream
1½ cups sugar	1 teaspoon vanilla
2 eggs, beaten	

Make topping first by mixing brown sugar, cinnamon and pecans. Set aside. Cream butter and sugar. Add eggs one at a time and mix well. Sift dry ingredients together; then add alternately with sour cream to butter mixture. Add vanilla. Pour ½ of batter into greased tube pan. Sprinkle ½ topping over batter. Add remaining batter, then sprinkle with balance of topping. Bake at 350° for 50 minutes. Cool on rack for 15 minutes before removing from pan.

SPOON BREAD

1 cup yellow cornmeal	1½ teaspoons salt
3 cups milk	2 tablespoons sugar
2 tablespoons butter	1 tablespoon baking powder
3 eggs	

Heat 2 cups of the milk, butter and meal until the butter is melted. Stir until smooth. Beat together eggs, salt and 1 cup milk. Add to hot meal mixture. Combine sugar and baking powder and add to mixture. Pour into greased 1½-quart casserole. Bake at 400° for 30-35 minutes. Serve hot with butter. Serves 8.

Favorite Easy Spoon Bread: Mix 1 8½-ounce box corn muffin mix; 1 cup sour cream; 2 eggs, beaten; 1 stick butter, melted; and 1 cup milk. Bake for 45 minutes to 1 hour at 350°.

A favorite with Southern cooks for many years, this "bread" originated from Indian porridge and is the consistency of porridge or pudding. Many recipes require beating egg whites and yolks separately but this one is quicker, delicious and more authentic ... a real favorite!!

SIX WEEKS BRAN MUFFINS

1 15-ounce box of raisin bran	1 teaspoon cinnamon
2½ cups sugar	1 cup cooking oil
5 cups flour	4 eggs, beaten
5 teaspoons soda	1 quart buttermilk
2 teaspoons salt	

Mix dry ingredients; add liquid ingredients and mix well. Store in covered plastic or glass container in the refrigerator and use as desired.

To use: Fill greased muffin tins ⅔ full. Bake at 400° for 18-20 minutes. Batter may be kept for 6 weeks. Do not freeze.

EASY TEA MUFFINS

1 stick butter, softened	2 cups Bisquick
8-ounce carton sour cream	

Stir sour cream and Bisquick into softened butter. Bake in greased miniature (do **not** use regular size) muffin tins at 350° for 15 minutes. Muffins will be soft in the middle. Makes about 30 miniature muffins.

Favorite Variation: Beer Muffins: Substitute 1 cup beer* and 1 tablespoon sugar for sour cream and butter. Stir all ingredients together and let stand at room temperature for 30 minutes. Don't stir again, but spoon into greased regular size muffin tins. Bake at 400° for 20-25 minutes. *Good use of left-over beer. For a sweeter beer muffin, use ¼ cup sugar.

FAVORITE CINNAMON TOAST MIX

3 teaspoons cinnamon	1 cup sugar

Mix thoroughly, and sprinkle on bread that has been spread with butter. Toast to a golden brown.

SWEETS

FRENCH APPLE TORTE

4 eggs	2 cups cooking apples, chopped
3 cups sugar	2 cups walnuts, chopped
8 tablespoons flour	2 teaspoons vanilla
5 teaspoons baking powder	½ teaspoon salt

Break eggs in bowl and beat with electric mixer until they are very frothy and lemon-colored (about 10-15 minutes). Fold in next seven ingredients in above order. When well mixed, pour into two well-buttered baking pans, 9 x 12-inches. Bake in 325° oven about 45 minutes, until crusty and brown. To serve, cut each into 8 segments, scoop up with pancake turner (keeping crusty side up), put on dessert plate and cover with whipped cream, flavored with vanilla and sugar. Top with a few chopped nuts. (Pecans may be substituted for walnuts.) Serves 16.

BLUEBERRY TORTE

1½ cups graham cracker crumbs	2 tablespoons lemon juice
½ cup butter	1 16½-ounce can blueberries,
2 cups sugar	drained
2 eggs	½ pint whipping cream, whipped
1 8-ounce package cream cheese	1 tablespoon sugar
5 tablespoons cornstarch	1 teaspoon vanilla

Combine crumbs, butter and ½ cup sugar. Mix and line 10-inch square pan. Beat eggs, ½ cup sugar and cream cheese until smooth. Spread over crumb crust and bake for 20 minutes at 350°. While this bakes, make topping. Blend cornstarch, 1 cup sugar, lemon juice and juice of blueberries. Cook until thick. Cool and add blueberries. Pour over baked mixture. Refrigerate. When ready to serve, top with whipped cream whipped with 1 tablespoon sugar and 1 teaspoon vanilla. Serves 10 to 12. Can be made a day ahead.

WORLD'S BEST LEMON SOUFFLE

8 eggs, room temperature	¾ cup fresh lemon juice
1 cup sugar	1 tablespoon grated lemon rind
2 packages unflavored gelatin	2 cups whipping cream, whipped

Beat the eggs and sugar together at highest speed of mixer for about 20 minutes, until creamy and light. While eggs are beating, soften gelatin in ¼ cup lemon juice. Warm slightly to dissolve the gelatin. Add dissolved gelatin to rest of the lemon juice. Reduce beating speed to slow and **very slowly** pour lemon juice into eggs. Add grated lemon rind. **Fold** in whipped cream and pour into a prepared souffle dish. Refrigerate 3-4 hours to congeal before serving. Remove the paper collar and decorate with whipped cream, lemon slices and mint. This freezes well but should be taken out of freezer and put in refrigerator about 3 hours before serving. This is a congealed dessert, not to be served as a frozen one. **To prepare souffle dish:** Put a wax paper collar around the outside of the souffle dish. Tie with string. Oil inside of collar with vegetable oil.

CHOCOLATE DELIGHT

¾ cup butter, melted
1½ cups flour
¾ cup pecans, finely chopped
  (optional)
1 8-ounce package cream cheese,
  softened
1 cup confectioners sugar
1 13½-ounce carton non-dairy
  whipped topping

1 3¾-ounce package vanilla instant
  pudding
1 4½-ounce package chocolate
  instant pudding
3 cups milk
Chopped pecans and grated
  chocolate to decorate

Combine butter, flour and pecans. Press into a 9 x 13-inch pan and bake at 375° for 15 minutes. Cool. Combine cream cheese, confectioners sugar and 1½ cups whipped topping. Spread over the cool crust and chill. Combine pudding mixes and milk. Beat 2 minutes with rotary mixer. Spread on top. Top with remaining whipped topping. Sprinkle with pecans and grated chocolate. Refrigerate. Serves 16.

Favorite Variations: Substitute 2 packages lemon instant pudding or 2 packages coconut cream instant pudding for the vanilla and chocolate. Change decorations on top to fit flavor . . . lemon slices or grated coconut.

PUMPKIN ROLL

3 eggs
1 cup sugar
1 teaspoon lemon juice
⅔ cup cooked pumpkin, mashed
¾ cup flour
2 teaspoons cinnamon
½ teaspoon nutmeg

2 teaspoons baking powder
1 teaspoon ginger
½ cup pecans, chopped
1¼ cup confectioners sugar
1 8-ounce package cream cheese
4 tablespoons butter, melted
1 teaspoon vanilla

Beat eggs until light and lemon-colored (about 10 minutes). Slowly add sugar and lemon juice. Fold in pumpkin. Sift flour, cinnamon, nutmeg, baking powder and ginger together and fold into egg mixture. Prepare 11x16-inch jelly roll pan by greasing bottom, covering bottom with waxed paper and buttering the waxed paper. Pour in mixture. Sprinkle with pecans. Bake at 350° for 15 minutes. Turn out on damp dishcloth that has been sprinkled with ¼ cup confectioners sugar. Roll up and cool. Prepare filling by beating together cream cheese, butter, vanilla and 1 cup confectioners sugar. Unroll pumpkin roll and spread with cream cheese mixture. Reroll and wrap in aluminum foil. Refrigerate several hours. Dust with confectioners sugar to serve. Freezes well.

FAVORITE CHOCOLATE TIPS

● To avoid white deposits on a chocolate cake, dust pan with cocoa instead of flour.

● When shaving chocolate for decorations, have chocolate at room temperature and use a vegetable-peeler for quick, easy results.

● In melting chocolate, it is best to melt over warm, not too hot water. Chocolate can scorch.

● If a recipe calls for a square of chocolate and you have none, substitute 4 tablespoons of cocoa and ½ teaspoon of butter.

MERINGUES

4 egg whites
½ teaspoon cream of tartar
1 cup sugar

1 teaspoon vanilla (optional)
A favorite filling

Beat room temperature egg whites with cream of tartar in a clean, dry mixing bowl. When peaks begin to form, add sugar and vanilla **very** slowly. It is important that the sugar has time to be completely absorbed and to liquify. When the beaters are removed, the peaks should stand **absolutely** straight up. The whites should be glossy but not dry. Line a cookie sheet with parchment paper or brown paper. Shape meringue in individual shells, pie crusts, large dessert shell or torte layers. Bake at 275° for one hour. Turn off oven; do not open and leave meringues in oven for 2 more hours.

Favorite Variation: Fold 1 cup chopped nuts into stiffly beaten egg whites.

Favorite Shapes: Individual Shells: Drop by tablespoons on the paper-lined cookie sheet. Hollow out the centers to ¼ inch thick, with the back of the spoon, to hold filling. Yields 20. **Pie Crusts:** Line two 9-inch pie pans with meringue and bake using the same method. **Large Dessert Shells:** Draw a 9-inch circle on the paper-lined cookie sheet. Spread evenly within circle about ¼ - ½ inch thick. Mound sides about 1½ inches high with a spoon or pipe a border with a pastry tube. **Torte Layers:** Draw two 7-inch circles on the brown paper and spread meringue evenly within circles. Bake and cool. Spread filling between two layers and frost like a 2-layer cake.

Favorite Fillings: Ice Cream, custards, whipping cream and **fresh fruits** are all excellent meringue fillings. **Heath Bar Filling or Topping:** Whip 1 cup whipping cream. Fold in a dash of salt, 6 crushed Heath bars (for easy crushing, freeze first) and 2 teaspoons rum. This makes enough to "frost" two torte layers or use it as a topping for coffee ice cream in shells or pie crusts. **Chocolate Angel Filling:** In double boiler combine 2 cups miniature marshmallows and ¾ cup milk. When marshmallows are melted, remove from heat, and add a 12-ounce package of semi-sweet chocolate bits. Stir until smooth. Lightly beat 4 egg yolks and gradually stir a little hot mixture into the yolks. Return yolks to hot mixture. Cook and stir about 3-5 minutes until mixture thickens. Remove from heat and stir in 2 tablespoons light rum. Chill about 2 hours; then, fold in 1 cup of whipped cream. Top with additional whipping cream, and garnish with shaved chocolate.

Helpful Hints: Meringues made ahead of time should be stored in a sealed container. If they become soft, reheat them in a 200° oven for 15-20 minutes; then, allow them to cool before serving.

OLD-FASHIONED AMBROSIA

1 dozen oranges
1 15¼-ounce can crushed pineapple

½ 7-ounce package frozen coconut

Peel, section and chop oranges. Add pineapple and juice along with coconut. Allow to stand overnight. Drain. Top with cherry.

Favorite Variation: Add sliced bananas.

TRIFLE

1 recipe Vanilla Custard	Favorite Pound Cake or 24 Lady
2 cups fresh fruit in season	Fingers
(peaches, strawberries, or	½ cup sherry
blueberries)	

Place a layer of pound cake slices in the bottom of an 8-inch crystal bowl. Sprinkle with ¼ cup of sherry. Add a layer of 1 cup of fruit. Next add a layer of ½ of the custard. Repeat these layers a second time. Refrigerate overnight or several hours. Before serving, top with whipping cream flavored with sugar and sherry.

There are almost as many variations of trifle as there are cookbooks. The basic ingredients have traditionally been cake, fruit, custard and sherry. Canned fruit is often used as well as nuts and even jams for variety (such as 1 cup apricot jam and toasted almonds). Experiment with **your** family's favorite fruit flavor.

Favorite Variation: Increase the sherry to 1 cup, omit the fruit, and you have **Tipsy Pudding.**

English Trifle is as old as America itself. Legend attributes its beginning to a creative English hostess who had no dessert for unexpected guests. She quickly made a simple custard and poured it over some rather stale, leftover cake which she had sprinkled with sherry and spread with jam. To add a touch of elegance, she put it in her best crystal bowl and topped it with whipped cream. When her guests complimented the delicious creation she ducked her head shyly and answered, "It's only a **trifle.***"*

VANILLA CUSTARD

1½ cups sugar	3 or 4 egg yolks
½ cup flour	3 cups milk
Pinch of salt	1 teaspoon vanilla

Combine sugar, flour and salt in top of double boiler. Beat egg yolks; stir in milk; add to sugar mixture, slowly. Cook over medium heat until thick, stirring constantly. Remove from heat; stir in vanilla. Cool. Strain or beat in blender if it has developed any lumps.

Favorite Variation: A favorite addition is 1 teaspoon almond extract. This custard is used as base for Banana Pudding, Tipsy Pudding or Trifle. Excellent served over fresh fruit and/or meringues.

ELEGANT ENDINGS FROM HUMBLE BEGINNINGS
(or Favorites with "Sto'-Bought" Ice Cream)

CHERRIES JUBILEE

2 16½-ounce cans Bing cherries	2 tablespoons water
⅓ cup currant jelly	½ to ¾ cup brandy
2 tablespoons cornstarch	1 quart vanilla ice cream

Scoop ice cream into large balls; freeze. Drain syrup from cherries and heat. Add jelly, cornstarch and water; mix well. Cook until thick. Add cherries and heat thoroughly. Heat brandy. Ignite brandy and pour over cherries; then spoon over ice cream.

ALMOND ELEGANCE

1 quart vanilla ice cream, softened
2 tablespoons orange juice
1 teaspoon almond extract
5 tablespoons toasted, slivered
  almonds
½ pint whipping cream, whipped
  (or 8-ounce carton non-dairy
  whipped topping)

1 10-ounce carton frozen
  strawberries
2 tablespoons orange juice
  concentrate
3 tablespoons powdered sugar

To the softened ice cream, add 2 tablespoons orange juice, almond extract and 2 tablespoons toasted almonds. Fold in the whipped cream. Freeze in individual molds. Heat the strawberries with the 2 tablespoons orange juice concentrate. Serve hot over unmolded ice cream. Before serving, sprinkle powdered sugar and 3 tablespoons toasted almonds on top.

FROZEN CARAMEL-PEACH DELIGHT

1½ cup fine graham cracker crumbs
¼ cup sugar
½ cup butter, melted
1 package (1 pound) frozen peach
  slices, thawed

2 pints vanilla ice cream
¼ cup butter, melted
½ cup brown sugar
½ cup pecans, chopped

In a large 10-inch pie plate or 9 x 9-inch pan, mix graham cracker crumbs and ¼ cup sugar. Add ½ cup melted butter. Mix well and press to line bottom and sides. Bake at 400° for 8-10 minutes. Chill. Drain peaches and save 1 tablespoon of the juice. Soften 1 pint ice cream and mix with ½ of the peach slices. Spread over crust and freeze. Mix together ¼ cup melted butter, brown sugar and the tablespoon of peach juice. Bring to a boil stirring constantly. Lower heat and cook slowly for 5 more minutes. Stir in ½ of the pecans. Cool slightly and spread on the ice cream. Mix remaining ice cream and peach slices. Spread over the pecan mixture. Sprinkle remaining pecans on top.

MUD PIE

1 box Famous chocolate wafers or
1 15-ounce package Oreos, crushed
⅔ cup butter, melted
½ gallon coffee ice cream
4 squares unsweetened chocolate

1 cup sugar
1 13 ounce can evaporated milk
2 tablespoons butter
Whipped cream
Nuts for topping

This makes 2 pies or can be put in one 9 x 13-inch pan. Make crust with chocolate cookies and ⅔ cup melted butter. Press in pan. Top with coffee ice cream. Freeze hard. Make chocolate sauce in double boiler. Mix the unsweetened chocolate, sugar, evaporated milk and butter. Cook until thick. Cool and pour over ice cream. Freeze. Serve pie with whipped cream and nuts.

Make your own coffee ice cream: Soften ½ gallon ice cream or ice milk. Add 2-3 tablespoons powdered instant coffee dissolved in 1 tablespoon vanilla and 1-2 tablespoons rum flavoring. Mix well. Refreeze in sealed container or use to make pie.

CHRISTMAS COOKIES

3 teaspoons soda
3 tablespoons milk
1 pound dates, chopped
1 pound candied cherries (½ green and ½ red), chopped
1 pound candied pineapple (⅓ white, ⅓ red, ⅓ green)
1 pound white raisins
3 cups pecans, chopped

3 cups flour
1 stick butter
1 cup light brown sugar
4 eggs
2 ounces brandy or bourbon
¾ teaspoon nutmeg, cake spice or cinnamon
1½ teaspoons vanilla

Dissolve soda in milk. Set aside. Roll chopped fruit and nuts in 1 cup of flour. Put aside. Cream butter and sugar. Add 1 egg at a time, beating thoroughly after each. Add bourbon, milk, remaining flour, spices and vanilla. Stir in fruit. (The batter is very stiff.) Drop by small teaspoons onto well-greased cookie sheets. Bake at 300° for 15 to 18 minutes. Remove from pans right away to cool on rack. These can be made quite a while ahead and frozen, and are better after storing.

Favorite Variation: Really pretty decorated with chopped cherries, but this takes an extra pound of red and green cherries.

SUPER-DUPER BROWNIES

1 cup *real* butter
3 tablespoons cocoa or 2 squares unsweetened chocolate
2 cups sugar
1½ cups pecans, chopped

1⅓ cups self-rising flour
2 teaspoons vanilla
4 eggs
2 cups miniature marshmallows

Melt butter* and sugar. Add all ingredients except eggs and marshmallows. Add eggs one at a time. Pour into greased, floured 9 x 13-inch pan. Bake at 350° for 35-40 minutes. For a "Basic Brownie," stop here; do not add marshmallows or icing. While hot, spread with 2 cups miniature marshmallows and chocolate icing. Put back in the oven for a few minutes and when warm, spread evenly. *If using chocolate squares, melt with butter.

Chocolate Icing

¼ cup butter
1 tablespoon cream
2 cups confectioners sugar

⅓ cup cocoa
¼ teaspoon salt

Bring butter and cream to boiling point. Add remaining ingredients to make spreading consistency — may need to use a little more or less sugar.

FAVORITE HINTS FOR COOKIES

● Store soft cookies in tightly covered container. If they begin to dry out, add a slice of apple to the container.

● Store crisp cookies in a loosely covered container. To "recrisp," bake for 3-5 minutes in a preheated 350° oven.

GINGERBREAD BOYS AND GIRLS

1 cup butter
1½ cups sugar
1 egg
1 tablespoon water or orange juice
2 tablespoons dark corn syrup or
   molasses
½ teaspoon salt

3¼ cups flour
2 teaspoons soda
2 teaspoons cinnamon
1 teaspoon ginger
¼ teaspoon ground cloves
1 teaspoon nutmeg

Cream butter and sugar. Add egg and beat well. Add water and syrup and mix. Sift dry ingredients together and add to creamed mixture. Mix well and chill at least 1 hour. Prepare a floured surface and roll out dough ⅛-¼-inch thick. Cut with cookie cutters. If using as tree ornaments, make hole with toothpick or dried bean before cooking. Before baking, place raisins for eyes, nose, mouth and buttons, or decorate later with Decorator Icing under Sugar Cookies after they are cooked and cooled. Place on an ungreased cookie sheet. Bake at 375° for 8 to 10 minutes.

SUGAR COOKIES
(Ornament Cookies)

1 stick butter
1 cup sugar
1 egg
1½ teaspoon vanilla

2 cups flour
1 teaspoon baking powder
½ teaspoon salt
Sugar for sprinkling tops

Cream butter and sugar; then add egg and vanilla. Sift dry ingredients together and add to other mixture. Chill at least 3 hours or overnight. Take out just enough to roll on floured surface. Leave the remainder in the refrigerator until ready to use. Cut out with cookie cutters. Bake on greased cookie sheet at 375° for 8 minutes. If not decorating, sprinkle immediately with sugar. Makes about 2 dozen depending on size of cookie. For variety, you may add ½ teaspoon lemon rind. Be sure to make hole in cookie before baking if it is to be used as a tree ornament. This may be done by inserting a broken toothpick or a dried bean where you want the hole or cutting a hole with a straw before baking. Watch carefully, as they burn easily. Cool before frosting. Frost with Decorator Icing.

Favorite Variation: To make chocolate cookies, add 4 tablespoons cocoa.

Decorator Icing for Christmas Sugar Cookies and Gingerbread Boys and Girls:

1 cup butter, softened
1 pound confectioners sugar, sifted
⅛ teaspoon salt

½ teaspoon vanilla
Food colorings

Beat butter and sugar until smooth. Add salt and vanilla. Beat. Divide into separate bowls and tint as desired. Use decorating tubes if available or decorate using toothpicks. If frosting becomes too stiff, add a few drops of water. It may be kept for several days in a sealed container in the refrigerator, then allowed to reach room temperature again before using.

For a white-white icing: Substitute about 3 tablespoons cream for the butter and use white vanilla or eliminate it.

LEMON BARS

1 cup butter	2 cups granulated sugar
1 scant cup confectioners sugar	1 teaspoon baking powder
2 cups flour	4 tablespoons flour
4 eggs, well beaten	8 tablespoons lemon juice

Cream butter, confectioners sugar and 2 cups flour. Put in 9 x 13-inch pan. Bake at 350° for 20 minutes. Remove from the oven and pour a mixture of the 5 remaining ingredients over the cooked shell. Bake at 325° for another 30-35 minutes. Sprinkle with confectioners sugar. Allow to cool before cutting and removing from pan. These also make a delicious dessert when cut in larger squares and topped with vanilla ice cream or whipped cream. Garnish with a thin twist of lemon and a sprig of mint.

M & M COOKIES OR CHOCOLATE CHIP COOKIES

1 cup brown sugar	1 teaspoon salt
1 cup granulated sugar	1 cup plain M & M candies
1 cup butter	1 cup rolled oats, uncooked
2 eggs	(optional)
2 teaspoons vanilla	1 cup shelled peanuts, roasted and
2¼ cups flour	unsalted (optional)
1 teaspoon soda	

Cream sugars and butter. Beat in eggs and vanilla. Sift dry ingredients together; add to sugar mixture and blend well. Stir in M & M's, oats and peanuts. (If you roast your own peanuts, be sure to remove red skins by rolling in your hands.) Drop teaspoonfuls on a greased cookie sheet. Bake at 375° for 10-12 minutes. Cool on wire rack. Makes 50-75 cookies.

Favorite Variation: Substitute 1 cup chopped pecans and 2 cups chocolate chips for M M's, oats and peanuts. An excellent chocolate chip cookie. And speaking of Chocolate Chip Cookies — try serving them different ways:

Giant Chocolate Chip Cookies: Scoop dough with ice cream scoop. Drop on greased cookie sheet. Mash with back of spoon into 5-inch circles. Bake according to directions.

Chocolate Chip Cookie "Cake": Bake in a 14-inch pizza pan. Line pan with aluminum foil for easy removal. Decorate with Decorator Icing and add candles. Serve by slicing or breaking off pieces. Children love this giant cookie!!

Chocolate Chip Cookie "Sundae": Top a giant cookie with vanilla ice cream and chocolate sauce. Add a little whipped cream on top and a cherry — you've created an irresistible sundae!

Chocolate "Chipwich": Sandwich ice cream (vanilla, chocolate or mint) between two chocolate chip cookies. Wrap in plastic wrap and freeze. Ready at a moment's notice for a fireside "picnic."

- Pizza cutter is the **best** brownie or bar cookie cutter.
- Bake cookies on middle rack of oven.

MELTING MOMENTS

1 cup soft butter
⅓ cup confectioners sugar

¾ cup cornstarch
1 cup cake flour

Icing

2 tablespoons melted butter
1 cup confectioners sugar
½ teaspoon lemon juice

½ teaspoon grated lemon rind
Light cream to make spreadable
2 drops yellow food coloring

Mix all cookie ingredients well — may use blender or food processor. Refrigerate 30 minutes. Roll into balls and place on lightly greased cookie sheet. Press in center and bake at 350° for 15 minutes. While still warm, ice with the above icing.

POUND CAKE WAFERS

2 sticks *real* butter
⅔ cup sugar
1 egg, beaten

1 teaspoon vanilla
2 cups flour
Pecan halves

Cream butter and sugar well. Add egg; then add vanilla and flour. Drop from teaspoon and press down in center with pecan half. Bake 350° on ungreased cookie sheet for about 15 minutes.

Favorite Variations: (1) Place cherry on top, or dampen finger and press cookie down in center and place small amount of jelly or preserves in indentation. (2) **Easy Bar Cookies:** Make above recipe but use 1 cup sugar and pat dough into 11 x 16-inch baking sheet with sides. Sprinkle top with ½ cup chopped pecans and mash into dough. Bake at 300° for 30 minutes or longer. Cut into bars.

REESE'S PEANUT BUTTER CUPS

1 refrigerator roll of sugar or peanut butter "slice and bake" cookies

36 Reese's miniature peanut butter cup candies

Cut cookie dough into 9 equal slices; cut each slice into fourths. Put one piece in each muffin cup of greased miniature muffin tins. Bake at 375° for 10 minutes. While they are in the oven, unwrap the candy. When the cookies are taken from the oven, **immediately** press one candy cup into the center of each hot cookie. Allow to cool in the pan for about 10 minutes. Remove carefully and place on a paper towel until cool. Children love to help with this.

SINFUL SEVEN-LAYER COOKIE

1 stick butter
1 cup crushed graham cracker crumbs
1 6-ounce package semi-sweet chocolate bits

1 6-ounce package butterscotch bits
1 cup Angelflake coconut
1 can sweetened condensed milk
1 cup pecans, chopped

Melt butter in 9 x 13-inch baking dish. Sprinkle other ingredients on top in order as they are listed. Do not stir or mix. Bake at 350° for 30 minutes. Allow to cool before cutting and removing from pan.

Favorite Variation: Eliminate butterscotch bits and pecans to make "Hello Dolly Cookies."

SNOWBIRD TRAIL BARS

1 cup butter	1 teaspoon soda
½ cup sugar	1½ cups rolled oats, uncooked
½ cup brown sugar	1 6-ounce package chocolate chips
2 eggs	1 cup pecans, broken
1 teaspoon vanilla	
1¼ cups flour	

Cream butter and sugars well. Blend in eggs and vanilla. Sift flour and soda together and add to first mixture. Stir in oats, chocolate chips and pecans. Bake 25-30 minutes at 375° in a well-greased 9 x 13-inch pan.

Nestled in the mountains of North Carolina near Robinsville is a picturesque hideaway, Snowbird Lodge. Their "Trail Bars" are a special treat packed in picnic lunches for all-day hikers . . . lots of added energy and oh-so-good!

FAVORITE HINTS FOR CAKES

● To keep fruit cakes from drying out, sprinkle with sherry or include an apple half in the cake tin.

● A light sprinkling of sugar on the cake plate prevents a freshly-baked cake from sticking.

● Grease only the bottoms of cake pans . . . not the sides.

● When baking cakes, have all ingredients at room temperature.

CARROT CAKE

1½ cups salad oil	2 teaspoons soda
2 cups sugar	1 teaspoon salt
4 eggs	3 cups raw carrots, grated
2 cups flour	½ cup pecans, chopped (optional)
2 teaspoons cinnamon	

Cream Cheese Icing

1 8-ounce package cream cheese	2 teaspoons vanilla
1 stick butter	½ cup pecans, chopped
1 box confectioners sugar, sifted	

Cream oil and sugar together. Add eggs one at a time. Mix dry ingredients, then stir into the egg mixture. Fold in pecans and carrots. Pour into 3 greased 8 or 9-inch layer pans and bake at 350° for 25-30 minutes (or in tube pan for 1 hour).

Icing: Have butter and cream cheese at room temperature. Cream together well. Add confectioners sugar and vanilla, beating well. Stir in pecans. Spread between layers and over cooled cake. Refrigerate. Freezes well.

YUMMY BANANA SPLIT CAKE

2 cups graham cracker crumbs
1 stick butter, melted
3 cups confectioners sugar
1 8-ounce package cream cheese
1 teaspoon vanilla

1 egg
4-5 bananas, sliced
1 cup crushed pineapple, drained
2 8-ounce cartons non-dairy
    whipped topping
½ cup pecans, chopped

Prepare crust by mixing finely crushed cracker crumbs and melted butter. Press on bottom of 9 x 13-inch pan. Reserve a few crumbs for garnish. Combine sugar, softened cream cheese, vanilla and egg and spread on crust. Add layer of bananas and drained pineapple. Cover with non-dairy whipped topping and sprinkle toasted pecans on top. Refrigerate 12 to 24 hours. Cut in squares. May be made in two 8-inch pie pans.

SENSATIONAL CHOCOLATE CAKE

1 cup cocoa
2 cups boiling water
2¾ cups flour
2 teaspoons baking soda
½ teaspoon salt

½ teaspoon baking powder
1 cup butter, softened
2½ cups sugar
4 eggs, room temperature
1½ teaspoons vanilla

Filling

1 cup heavy cream, whipped
¼ cup confectioners sugar

1 teaspoon vanilla

Frosting

6-ounce package semi-sweet
    chocolate morsels
½ cup light cream

1 cup butter
3½ cups confectioners sugar
1 teaspoon vanilla

Mix cocoa and boiling water. Mix with whisk until smooth. Cool completely. Mix dry ingredients, set aside. In large bowl, beat at high speed the butter, sugar, eggs and vanilla. Beat until light, about 5 minutes. Add dry ingredients alternately with cocoa mixture in halves — beginning and ending with flour. Beat only until well mixed; do not overbeat. Pour into 3 greased and floured 9-inch layer cake pans. Bake at 350° for 25 to 30 minutes. Cool on racks for 10 minutes; then carefully remove from pans. Cool completely.

To make filling: Whip cream with sugar and vanilla and refrigerate. To assemble cake, place cake layer top side down on cake plate. Spread with half the whipped cream. Place second layer top side down. Spread with remainder of whipped cream. Place third layer top side **up.** Frost sides and top with chocolate frosting. Keep refrigerated. Serves 12 or more. This cake is moist, light and sinfully rich, but well worth the effort. Follow the recipe exactly. Make no substitutions.

To make frosting: Combine chocolate morsels, cream and butter in medium saucepan. Stir over medium heat until smooth. Remove from heat. Blend in sifted confectioners sugar and vanilla. Beat until it holds its shape (set bowl in ice if necessary).

ICE-BOX COCONUT CAKE

1 box 2-layer white cake mix	2 cups sugar
2 8-ounce cartons sour cream	1 12-ounce carton non-dairy
2 7-ounce packages frozen coconut	whipped topping

Make white cake by package instructions and cool completely. Cut each layer in half horizontally, making 4 layers. Make filling by combining sour cream, coconut and sugar. Mix well and pour filling between each layer. Frost cake completely with whipped topping. Reserve a little coconut to sprinkle on top for decoration. Place in sealed container in refrigerator for several days before serving. UNBELIEVABLE!!

Favorite Variation: Make cake mix in 9 x 13-inch pan. While it is still hot, punch holes in the top with a fork. Pour over the cake a mixture of 1 can sweetened condensed milk and 1 5-ounce can coconut creme. Top with an 8-ounce carton non-dairy whipped topping and sprinkle with coconut.

PRIZE FRUIT CAKE

1 pound candied cherries	1 teaspoon nutmeg
1 pound candied pineapple	4 cups flour
½ cup bourbon or sherry	1 teaspoon baking powder
2 sticks butter	½ teaspoon salt
1 cup sugar	2½ cups shelled pecans
6 eggs	

Let fruit soak overnight in the bourbon or sherry. Cream butter and sugar. Beat in eggs one at a time, beating thoroughly until four eggs have been added. Add nutmeg and a little flour. Then alternating, add the other two eggs and the flour that is already thoroughly mixed with salt and baking powder. Fold nuts and soaked fruit into the batter. Mix thoroughly. Pour into 2 loaf pans, lined with greased brown paper. Bake at 250° for 2 hours. To prevent drying, place a small pan of water in the oven during baking. If cake still seems dry, pour a little bourbon or sherry on top. Stored in a cool place in a sealed cake tin, this cake keeps for a long time.

SURPRISE CAKE

1 cup flour	½ cup butter
½ cup light brown sugar	Pinch salt

Filling

1 cup light brown sugar	1½ cups coconut, grated
2 tablespoons flour	1 cup pecans, chopped
½ teaspoon baking powder	3 eggs, unbeaten
1 teaspoon vanilla	Pinch salt

Mix first four ingredients. Spread in 7 x 11-inch pan and cook 10 minutes at 400°. Mix filling well and spread on first mixture. Bake 30 minutes at 375°. Cut in squares to serve. Great addition to a tray of fruit cake and pound cake slices to accompany ambrosia.

FAVORITE POUND CAKE

2 sticks *real* butter, softened
½ cup Crisco
3 cups sugar
5 eggs
3 cups flour
½ teaspoon baking powder

⅛ teaspoon salt
1 cup milk
2 teaspoons vanilla
1 teaspoon almond extract
(optional)

Have all ingredients at room temperature. Cream butter, Crisco and sugar. Add eggs one at a time, beating after each egg. Sift dry ingredients together. Mix milk with flavoring. Beginning and ending with dry ingredients, alternate adding them and milk to the creamed mixture. Mix well but do not overbeat. Put in well-greased and floured tube pan. Bake at 325° for 1 hour and 15 minutes. Leave in pan for 30 minutes.

WILLIAMSBURG POUND CAKE

Add ⅛ teaspoon mace and ⅛ teaspoon nutmeg to Favorite Pound Cake. Eliminate almond extract. Serve with Eggnog Topping.

Eggnog Topping: Beat 1 egg in top of double boiler. Add 1⅓ cups sweetened condensed milk, stirring constantly, and cook 10 minutes. Don't let water boil. Remove from heat and add ½ teaspoon rum and ¼ teaspoon nutmeg. Fold in 1 cup whipping cream, whipped. Serve warm or cold over pound cake, fruitcake or other fruit desserts.

CHOCOLATE POUND CAKE

Add 4 tablespoons cocoa to dry ingredients for **Favorite Pound Cake.** Be sure to use the almond extract for this one. Frost with Chocolate Glaze.

Chocolate Glaze: Combine 2¼ cups sifted confectioners sugar and 3 tablespoons cocoa. Add ¼ cup softened butter and 4 tablespoons milk. Beat until smooth. Pour glaze on cake while it is still hot.

MAPLE-BROWN SUGAR POUND CAKE

Substitute 1 teaspoon maple flavoring for the almond extract in **Favorite Pound Cake.** Use 2 cups brown sugar and only 1 cup regular white sugar. Frost with Caramel Frosting.

Caramel Frosting: Melt ½ stick butter and ½ cup brown sugar over low heat. Boil 2 minutes, stirring constantly. Remove from heat and stir in 3 tablespoons milk. Return to heat; bring to a slow boil and add ¾ cup sifted confectioners sugar. Remove from heat and beat until smooth. Cool and spread evenly on cake or pour on hot cake as a glaze.

FESTIVE SPICE CAKE

1 8.5-ounce box spice cake mix
1 pint whipping cream, whipped
1 cup pecans, broken

½ cup green maraschino cherries, chopped
½ cup red maraschino cherries, chopped

Make spice cake according to directions. Put in 3 8-inch cake pans to bake. When cool, frost entire cake with mixture of whipped cream, nuts and cherries. Reserve a few whole nuts and cherries for decoration. (A 16-ounce carton of non-dairy whipped topping may be substituted for the whipped cream.) Keep refrigerated until ready to serve. Cake layers may be made ahead and frozen. Assemble and frost the day it is to be eaten.

FOUR STAR BOURBON BALLS

1 cup vanilla wafer crumbs, very fine	2 tablespoons cocoa
	¼ cup bourbon whiskey
1 cup pecans, chopped	1½ tablespoons white corn syrup
1 cup confectioners sugar	Enough confectioners sugar to coat

Mix vanilla wafer crumbs, pecans, confectioners sugar and cocoa. Mix bourbon and corn syrup together then add to crumb mixture. Form into small balls and roll in powdered sugar. Keep refrigerated until ready to serve.

DIVINE DIVINITY

¼ cup white corn syrup	2 egg whites, stiffly beaten
2½ cups sugar	1 teaspoon vanilla
¾ cup water	½ cup pecans, chopped

Mix syrup, sugar, and water in a saucepan. Cook over low heat, stirring constantly until mixture boils. Boil slowly without stirring until mixture forms hard balls when dropped in cold water (266 degrees). **Slowly** pour mixture over stiffly beaten egg whites, beating constantly. Continue to beat until mixture is very stiff. Fold in vanilla and pecans. Drop by teaspoons on waxed paper. Let stand until firm.

FAVORITE FOOL-PROOF FUDGE

5 cups sugar	1 7-ounce jar marshmallow cream
2 sticks butter	1 tablespoon vanilla
1 13-ounce can evaporated milk	2 cups pecans, chopped
3 6-ounce packages semi-sweet chocolate morsels	

Dissolve the sugar, butter and milk in a saucepan over medium heat, stirring constantly. Bring to a boil and boil exactly 9 minutes. Continue stirring. Remove from heat. Add chocolate chips and marshmallow cream. Stir until melted, then add vanilla and nuts. Pour into buttered 11 x 15-inch pan (jelly roll pan). Makes 5 pounds.

SUGARED PECANS

1 cup sugar	1 teaspoon vanilla
6 tablespoons milk	2 cups pecan halves
Dash salt	

Combine sugar, milk and salt in saucepan. Stir over low heat until mixture comes to a boil. Boil slowly until it forms a soft ball in cold water (234°). Add vanilla, then pecans and toss quickly. Pour on waxed paper. Work quickly to separate into single halves or small clusters. Cool.

MISSISSIPPI BLACK BOTTOM PIE

14 chocolate ginger snaps or other
  chocolate cookies
5 tablespoons butter, melted
2 cups milk, scalded
4 eggs, separated
1 cup sugar
1¼ tablespoons cornstarch

1½ squares chocolate, unsweetened
1 teaspoon vanilla
1 envelope gelatin
4 tablespoons water
¼ teaspoon cream of tartar
2 tablespoons rum
1 cup whipping cream, whipped

Make crust of chocolate cookies and butter. Bake at 300° for 10 minutes. Put 2 cups scalded milk in double boiler and *slowly* add 4 beaten egg yolks. Then mix ½ cup sugar and cornstarch and add to eggs and milk. Cook until it coats spoon. To 1 cup of the custard add 1½ squares chocolate and 1 teaspoon vanilla. Cool. Soak gelatin in 4 tablespoons cold water. Add to rest of custard. Cool. Fold egg whites (4), beaten with ½ cup sugar, cream of tartar and rum into vanilla custard. Put chocolate mixture in crust. Add rum custard and put in refrigerator. When ready to serve, put 1 cup flavored and sweetened whipped cream on top and grate chocolate over the top.

FAVORITE BLUEBERRY PIE

1 baked pie shell (deep)
1 8-ounce package cream cheese
¾ cup powdered sugar
½ cup pecans, chopped

1 can blueberry pie filling
½ package gelatin
¼ cup water
Cool Whip

Mix cream cheese and powdered sugar. Spread in baked pie shell. Sprinkle with pecans. Heat blueberry pie filling. Soak gelatin in water and add to pie filling. Pour into pie shell. Chill overnight. Top with Cool Whip or flavored and sweetened whipped cream.

LIGHT AND LUSCIOUS ICE BOX PIE

1 9-ounce non dairy whipped
  topping
2 graham cracker crusts
1 can Eagle Brand condensed milk
1 8-ounce can crushed pineapple,
  drained

½ cup pecans, broken
½ cup coconut, grated
Small jar Maraschino cherries
2 tablespoons lemon juice

Combine condensed milk, pineapple, pecans, coconut and lemon juice. Fold in whipped topping. Spread in two crusts, and top with cherry halves. Chill for two hours before slicing.

MAPLE PECAN PIE

1 10″ pie shell, unbaked
½ cup butter
½ cup sugar
¾ cup white corn syrup

¼ cup maple syrup
3 eggs, slightly beaten
1 teaspoon vanilla
2 cups pecans, broken

Cream butter and sugar until light. Slowly stir in syrups; then add eggs and vanilla. Stir to blend and fold in pecans. Pour into chilled, unbaked pie shell. Bake at 325° for 1 hour. Makes 1 pie or 12 to 15 individual tarts.

PUMPKIN CHIFFON PIE

1 pie shell, baked
36 marshmallows
2 cups pumpkin, cooked and
    mashed

1 teaspoon pumpkin pie spice
1½ cups cream, whipped

Make and bake pie shell. Melt marshmallows in double boiler, and fold in pumpkin, pumpkin pie spice and 1 cup whipped cream. Chill and top with ½ cup whipped cream.

RITZ CRACKER PIE

20 Ritz crackers, crushed
½ cup sugar
1 teaspoon baking powder
1 cup nuts, pecans chopped
3 egg whites, beaten stiff

¼ cup plus 2 tablespoons sugar
1 tablespoon vanilla
1 8-ounce non dairy whipped
    topping or whipped cream
Grated Chocolate (optional)

Mix crackers, sugar and baking powder with nuts and set aside. Mix egg whites and sugar slowly. Combine with previous mixture. Pour into a greased Pyrex pie pan. Bake at 350° for 30 minutes. Cool before spreading top with non dairy whipped topping or whipped cream. Grated chocolate may be sprinkled over the whipped cream.

TEA TIME TASSIES

1 large egg
1 cup brown sugar
1 tablespoon butter, softened
1 recipe Cream Cheese Tart Pastry

1 teaspoon vanilla
Pinch salt
1¼ cups pecans, finely chopped

Mix filling ingredients using only ½ of the pecans. Line small muffin tins with pastry. Place 1 teaspoon filling in each tart shell. Sprinkle remaining chopped pecans on top. Bake at 325° for 25 minutes.

CREAM CHEESE TART PASTRY

1 3-ounce package cream cheese
1 cup flour

1 stick butter

Blend pastry ingredients. Chill dough for several hours. For tarts, shape dough into 36 one-inch balls and press each into ungreased muffin tins of the smallest size. Press dough with thumb to cover sides of tins. Fill with favorite filling. Bake at 325° for 25 minutes. Cool and remove from pans. Makes 3 dozen tarts or crust for one 9-inch pie. (If fillings do not need to be cooked, prebake unfilled tart shells at 400° for 10 minutes.) Cool before filling.

FAVORITE SWEET TIPS

● A few drops of lemon juice added to well-chilled whipping cream makes it whip faster and gives it more body.

● If you love pecan pie but want to save money, substitute crushed cornflakes for nuts. They will rise to the top and give a delicious flavor and crunchy surface.

● To prevent crust from becoming soggy when making a cream pie, sprinkle crust with powdered sugar.

BEVERAGES

INSTANT HOT CHOCOLATE MIX

1 pound box Nestle Quick
6 cups instant non-fat dry milk
¼ cup powdered sugar

1 cup non-dairy creamer
Marshmallows

Mix all ingredients except marshmallows in large container. Keep sealed until ready to use. Make hot chocolate by filling cup ⅓ full with mix. Add hot water to fill cup. Keep on hand for the holidays. Makes lots — depending on size of cups. Top with a marshmallow or a marshmallow rolled in cinnamon.

Favorite Variation: For a mocha taste, add ½-1 teaspoon of instant coffee to the cup of hot chocolate.

INSTANT RUSSIAN TEA MIX

1 1-pound, 2-ounce jar Tang
¾ cup instant tea with lemon
1½-2 cups sugar

1 teaspoon ground cloves
½-1 teaspoon cinnamon
½ teaspoon allspice

Mix all ingredients well. Store in tight container. To serve, use 2 teaspoons to a tea cup of boiling water.

BANANA CRUSH PUNCH

4 cups sugar
6 cups water
1 46-ounce can sweetened
    pineapple juice
2 12-ounce cans frozen orange juice
    concentrate, thawed

1½ cups lemon juice
6 ripe bananas, mashed
6 28-ounce bottles lemon-lime
    carbonated beverage or ginger
    ale

Dissolve sugar in water; add juices and mashed bananas. Mix everything except carbonated beverage. Divide into 6 equal portions in 6 freezer cartons and freeze ahead of time. Take out about 2 hours before serving time. Mix 1 portion with 1 bottle of ginger ale. Makes about 72 punch cup servings of slushy-type punch. No extra ice needed.

HOT CIDER PUNCH

6 cups apple juice
¼ cup honey
3 tablespoons lemon juice
1 20-ounce can unsweetened
    pineapple juice (2½ cups)

1 teaspoon lemon rind
¼ teaspoon nutmeg
Cinnamon stick
Orange studded with cloves

Boil juices and cinnamon. Simmer, covered, for 5 minutes. Add remaining ingredients, except orange, to boiling juices and simmer 5 more minutes uncovered. Makes 20 cups. To make orange: Heat oven to 325°. Place orange with cloves in baking pan with a little water and bake for 3 minutes. Float this in punch bowl with cinnamon stick, or put stick through orange. (Use potato peeler to make hole.)

MOCK DAIQUIRI SLUSHY

1 6-ounce can frozen lemonade
concentrate

1 fifth of sherry (inexpensive is
adequate)

Mix; place in a 32-ounce plastic container and place in freezer for several hours. Serves 6-8.

Favorite Variation: 3 6-ounce cans frozen lemonade, undiluted, 2 fifths Rosé wine, 2 28-ounce bottles of sparkling water. Serves 25.

WHISKEY SOUR PUNCH

1 quart lemonade
1 quart orange juice

1 quart whiskey — bourbon
2 quarts soda water

Pour over ice and add a cherry to each glass. Serves 50.

HOLIDAY EGGNOG

6 eggs
¾ cup sugar
1 pint whipping cream

1 pint bourbon
1 pint milk
1 jigger rum

Beat yolks separately with ¼ cup of the sugar. Beat whites with ½ cup sugar. Whip cream. Fold whites and cream into egg yolks mixture. Add whiskey; then last, pour in milk and rum, stirring constantly.

HOT BUTTERED RUM

2 sticks butter, softened
1 cup light brown sugar
1 cup confectioners sugar
1 teaspoon cinnamon
1 teaspoon nutmeg

½ quart vanilla ice cream, softened
Light rum
Whipped cream
Cinnamon sticks

Remove ice cream from freezer and allow to soften. Meanwhile, combine butter, sugars and spices, and beat until light and fluffy. Thoroughly mix with softened ice cream until blended. Return mixture to freezer. To serve, allow to soften slightly. Place 3 tablespoons butter mixture and 1 jigger of rum in a large mug. Fill with boiling water, and stir well. Top with whipped cream, and stir with cinnamon stick stirrers. Yield: about 12 cups.

IRISH COFFEE

1 cup strong coffee
1 teaspoon sugar
1 large scoop coffee ice cream

1 jigger Irish Whiskey
1 large dollop of whipped cream

Chill silver mint julep cups. Make strong coffee, adding 1 teaspoon sugar per cup while hot. Cool. Fill cup with scoop of coffee ice cream, one jigger of Irish Whiskey and coffee to within one inch of the top. Top with whipped cream. Serve with iced teaspoon and cookie for dessert. Recipe for one cup.

OTHER CHRISTMAS FAVORITES

Recipe or Idea	Source-Book	Page

OTHER CHRISTMAS FAVORITES

Recipe or Idea	Source-Book	Page

OTHER CHRISTMAS FAVORITES

Recipe or Idea	Source-Book	Page

OTHER CHRISTMAS FAVORITES

Recipe or Idea	Source-Book	Page

OTHER CHRISTMAS FAVORITES

Recipe or Idea	Source-Book	Page

CHRISTMAS NOTES

CHRISTMAS NOTES

CHRISTMAS NOTES

CHRISTMAS NOTES

INDEX

Index

Christmas Favorites
P.O. Box 15162
Charlotte, N.C. 28211

Please send me _____ copies of **Christmas Favorites**

Soft cover @ $6.95 each _____

Hard board cover @ $8.95 each _____

Shipping & handling @ $1.50 each _____

N.C. Residents: Add 6% tax per book _____

Total _____

Name _____

Address _____

City _____ State _____ Zip _____

If you would like a gift copy sent to another address, please include complete name and address. (   ) Enclose gift card from _____

Make check or money order payable to "Christmas Favorites."

- -

Christmas Favorites
P.O. Box 15162
Charlotte, N.C. 28211

Please send me _____ copies of **Christmas Favorites**

Soft cover @ $6.95 each _____

Hard board cover @ $8.95 each _____

Shipping & handling @ $1.50 each _____

N.C. Residents: Add 6% tax per book _____

Total _____

Name _____

Address _____

City _____ State _____ Zip _____

If you would like a gift copy sent to another address, please include complete name and address. (   ) Enclose gift card from _____

Make check or money order payable to "Christmas Favorites."

Please list any gift or Christmas shops in your area that might be interested in **CHRISTMAS FAVORITES.**

Name_____

Address_____

Telephone Number_____

City_____State_____Zip_____

Please list any gift or Christmas shops in your area that might be interested in **CHRISTMAS FAVORITES.**

Name_____

Address_____

Telephone Number_____

City_____State_____Zip_____

Please list any gift or Christmas shops in your area that might be interested in **CHRISTMAS FAVORITES.**

Name_____

Address_____

Telephone Number_____

City_____State_____Zip_____